HEART & DESIRE

Cheryl L. Howard

HEART & DESIRE

An Olympian's Journey of Faith

Cheryl Howard

HEART & DESIRE
by Cheryl Howard

International Standard Book Number

1-894928-60-1

Dedication

*This book is dedicated to my family and friends who
have supported and encouraged me
to press on to run the race of faith
that God has set before me,
to athletes, coaches, teachers,
home school moms and horse lovers
who share in my story of the heart,
and to those seeking to know the one true God.*

Contents

Clarifications & Acknowledgements

Heart and Desire is a book that has been four years in the making. It is an expression of who I am, beginning with my life as a child and continuing on until the present time. My early childhood began with a passion for horses, which was then replaced with competitive sports and, in the last twenty-five years, with a passion to know God in a deeper way.

This book is not about Natural Horsemanship in itself, but about the many lessons I learned from my relationship with my horse, Rocky, while applying Natural Horsemanship principles. I am not a horse trainer, nor an expert in Natural Horsemanship, therefore, I cannot take credit for any of the training concepts offered or explained. You may have heard of the 'Horse Whisperer,' Monty Roberts, and Pat Parelli. All of these people use Natural Horsemanship techniques to train horses. Horses, and in general, all challenges, have a way of developing your character, proving your motives, and teaching you lessons for life.

My first credit for the inspiration to write "Heart and Desire" goes to my Creator. God knew how to get my attention and answered the cries of my heart—to know Him and to walk in freedom from fear and failure. His precious gift of grace has enabled me to venture through life's challenges and come out stronger in spirit and leadership.

It is with great appreciation and love that I want to thank the people who stood alongside me for endless hours with patient encouragement, offering me emotional and physical support. The person who spent the most time with Rocky and I was Susan Warner. She is a horse trainer on Vancouver Island, gifted in the art of natural horsemanship. God chose to work through Susan's vast knowledge and experiences, her strong and fun loving character, and most of all her friendship, to reveal to me wonderful lessons in life. For a time, Leslie King assisted Susan during the initial training with Rocky. I am forever grateful to both of them.

Behind the scenes my close friends, Donna Anderson, Dan and Penny Galliazzo, Lorri Frandsen and Betty Parlee, and my family members—my husband, Tom, and children, Francine, Courtney, Andrew and Grace—gave me constant support and encouragement. I received additional outside information and inspiration from Pat Parelli's *Natural Horsemanship Manual* and Monty Robert's book, *The Man Who Listens to Horses*.

Prologue

Head and tail held high, nostrils flaring, red, sleek, glistening fur steaming in the morning hot sun; this is the lone black stallion after a long hard run. His hooves thunder out a message of power and independence as dust clouds envelop his awesome frame. He stands tense and quivering, ready to turn and race across the open range at the slightest hint of movement or sound. He is driven to flee his predators by instinctive fear. Forever the wild and free creature is vulnerable to his harsh climatic and environmental conditions. Disease, injury, sickness and shortage of food and water all pose constant threat to his survival. He knows little comfort or rest for more than a few moments of time. What is his purpose and destiny?

On the horizon he spots a large movement cresting the barren hill. His heart begins to beat wildly and his whole body is erect as he watches in anticipation a herd of nervous mares approaching his direction. Do they see him? Across the ridge a loud ninny echoes towards him. He snorts and ninnies a greeting in reply. Yes, they sense his presence and move in to circle him excitedly. Soon dust is flying with skittering bodies, heels kicking, mares squealing, biting and bucking, while the stallion proudly prances a dance around them showing off his prowess. When all is settled, the stallion takes his place as the Alpha horse leading the pack across the ridge. They move with purpose and harmony to higher ground where the entire rangeland can be surveyed. The free and wild stallion and his mares have found their identity, purpose and destiny in life. Or have they?

1.

My First Love

*E*veryone is born with a passion for something. As far back as I can remember my passion was for horses—any horse, even the old gray mares. My favorite television shows were westerns, just so I could see horses. The pony rides in Vancouver's Stanley Park were a must for me even if they were mechanical and short. I once had a childhood photo taken in the studio on a fake horse. If I couldn't ride a horse then it was enough just to look at one, smell the fur of one, or touch one's soft velvety nose and run my hands over its altogether lovely and strong body. And worse yet, if I couldn't see one or touch one then I would buy horse stories, color and draw horses and collect horse pictures. Anything horsy was for me.

Needless to say, I also loved horsing around with my neighborhood friends, playing Cowboys and Indians and horse and rider. I loved it when my step-dad gave me horse rides in the living room. One special childhood memory is of when my two brothers, my oldest sister and I stayed for a few weeks at my Nana and Granddad's lovely mountain estate in Haney. The neighbor's large draft horse, Queeny, was allowed to wander the mountain and I had the opportunity to ride her. Sometimes three of us sat on her at one time, riding without assistance! What a delightful experience, sitting on a horse in the rugged mountains. Horses brought mystery, romance and adventure to my life, all wrapped up in one.

Me on my rocking horse at 3 years old (1956)

Our family of seven children never owned a horse, but that didn't stop me from finding one to ride. Looking back now, it seemed that God must have planned a very special horse for me, for when I was three, we moved from Vancouver to a rural area of Richmond. When I was in elementary school a horse came to live in a field adjacent to our backyard. Maverick was a wonderful Mustang pony. His long flowing mane and tail were so rich that I could brush them all day and never untangle all the knots and burrs. I didn't even mind the thick dander and flies on his shiny reddish brown coat because it was all part of this dream horse I could secretly enjoy.

He was built like a magnificent Native Indian war pony. I was so fascinated with him that I eventually managed to persuade Maverick to let me sit on his back. He tolerated my constant intrusion into his pastoral life because I gave him fresh vegetables and apples from our garden and spent hours just petting him softly, hugging him gently, and whispering in his delicate ears. It didn't take me long to figure out how to get a free ride using a little string as reins and a fence rail for a boost. Bareback riding at a trot was a great challenge for me as I struggled to hang on to his thick mane. Sometimes he would be enticed to trot when a friend would run alongside the fence with a carrot. Doubling was even more fun as we jiggled along trying to hold on to each other. All was fine and dandy until I got surprisingly bucked off into the bramble bush and later, knocked off by an overhead branch. Instead of being discouraged I just kept finding more ways to ride this pony, never wanting to ask the owners if I could ride in case they would say no.

One day the inevitable shock came. Maverick's owners discovered my shenanigans and put a stop to my bareback riding without permission. Though my days of riding at liberty were over, I held on to the dream of owning not just one horse, but many! I thank God for giving me a taste of the desire of my heart right at the beginning of my turbulent childhood—a childhood in a blended family with many relationship problems.

2.

Pursuit of Excellence
& Shattered Dreams

*W*hen I was in grade six something else wonderful happened to me. Everyone started to talk about me, notice me and look up to me. I had talent, raw talent that I didn't know existed until I competed in my first school Sports Day. No one my age could run as fast or as far as me. My legs seemed to always reach the finish line first. Even in long jump or high jump my legs carried me beyond my classmates, who affectionately nicknamed me 'beanpole.'

At twelve years of age my family moved near Richmond center, within jogging distance of Minoru track where my brother Kirk and sister Marie were involved in the Richmond Track Club. In grade seven there came an opportunity for me to enter an important race, the Richmond Cross-Country Championships. I had no training or assistance before entering the race. (Actually, I was secretly smoking cigarettes at the time, which most certainly would have hampered my breathing.) What a surprise when I placed fourth! No more cigarette packages under the mattress!

This effortless achievement was the beginning of a new life for me. I found a route to success that I immensely enjoyed. Praise was finally coming to me by way of my peers and teachers. My picture was often in the Richmond newspaper and I usually won a prestigious award in school athletics. That year my parents allowed me to join the Richmond Track Club. My coach, Doug Clement, became my greatest role model and encourager. Over time I encountered many difficulties, such as chronic knee pain, back pain and stomach pain. The stress of performance in training and racing was constant as I focused on middle distance running (800-1500 meters) for my future career. My coach helped me progress from top Richmond age class mile champion to B.C. high school mile champion, to a high-ranking age class athlete. I had several Canadian records by the end of my high school years. As a teen, I must have competed close to a hundred times in one year.

Off to Canada Games in Halifax (1969)

My only taste of international competition during that time was at the end of my grade twelve year in 1971, when my brave and wonderful coach and his energetic gifted wife, Diane, took a group of us Kajak athletes (Richmond Track Club) on a month-long track tour to several European countries. It was in Amsterdam that I met my future husband, Tom. We had a wonderful time together in Europe, traveling and competing, and most of all, getting to know each other. There were many chuckles and jokes from our peers about our romantic encounter in Europe and the matching of us two together in Graz, Austria at a billet. Two years later we were married. A fast 1500-meter race in Verona, Italy, where I placed third against the current world record holder, showed me that I had potential for future international success. I won three bottles of wine in that race and faithfully brought them home for gifts.

In the fall, I entered the University of British Columbia and joined the track team under coach Lionel Pugh, a man who knew how to get under anyone's skin. During hard training my knees screamed out to me to stop and my stomach pains became chronic. My glory years of competitive track were quickly waning. Eventually, severe stomach pains forced me to drop out of some university cross-country races. I was so embarrassed! I had trained all through the previous seven years with chronic pain and discomfort, but could go on no longer.

No one, not even the specialists, could diagnose my stomach problems. My knees would periodically hold me back too, but I rarely let pain be a deterrent. Was it stress related? Was I burned out? I loved training and racing. (Twenty years later I discovered I had a milk intolerance, which would have greatly affected my stomach and energy level). I hadn't reached my goal of being the best middle distance runner in Canada. How could I give up the most important love of my life? I was a runner! I was not a quitter! What was happening to my heart and desire?

Hope would have continued to wane but for a critical turn of events that occurred while I was still in university. During that period of disillusionment I ran into a fellow student, Rhonda Ross. As I shared with her my utter discouragement and shattered dreams, she shared with me her new direction in competitive sports. She had switched from competitive swimming to rowing.

"Rowing? What's that?" I asked in ignorance. She briefly explained to me the sport of rowing. "I'm not terribly impressed at the thought of sitting down in a sport where there is no running," I responded. I asked her why she chose rowing over her swimming career. She enthusiastically responded that there was a campaign to promote women's rowing because of the up and coming '76 Olympics to be hosted in Montreal. Tricia Smith, Joy Fera, Rhonda Ross and several other young fit athletes had joined the Vancouver Rowing Club at Coal Harbor with hopes of gaining a berth on the Canadian Olympic team. I was intrigued!

3.

A Turn of Events

It was in 1974, the year after I married distance runner Tom Howard, that I started my rowing training on a huge barge rigged with oarlocks for rowing. The coach would walk up and down the barge barking out commands, mostly correcting our rowing technique. As a skinny athlete I was no match for the typical heavy weight and muscle bound rower who was expected to pull hard on long sweep oars in the ocean waves.

Thus I began a long arduous journey of daily weight training, one-legged squats, repetitive skipping, calisthenics, and some rowing. Winter training was bleak as we worked out in the leaky, dark old boathouse at the Vancouver Rowing Club. Our veteran Olympic coach, Laurie West, was a grueling coach who sentenced us to rigorous dry land training for many months. For a warm-up before training I would run down to Stanley Park from our Kitsilano apartment and return for the warm-down. The rowing training had strengthened the muscles and connective tissue around my knees so that I could run again. But rather than return to running, I chose to focus on rowing as my new sport to compete in at an international level. Little did I know what challenges would arise over the next four years.

Not long into my dry land training I decided to quit. It was far too frustrating and agonizing to train in such an unfamiliar fashion—building body mass and anaerobic power with little actual experience rowing in a real rowing shell. It was all so absurd. What were we doing? My light 5 foot 8 inch frame of 120 pounds was not much of a match to a typical rower's build of 160 pounds at 5 foot 10 inches or more. I was stretched beyond my limits, or was I? Where was my heart and desire now? It was quickly waning again. How could I keep up this mad pace of training for three years?

Early rowing days in a single scull

My husband, Tom, was my greatest source of inspiration, support and encouragement. He stated emphatically to me, "You can do it. It will get easier. You've just started, so give it time." Well, I can assure you that I came to this same despairing conclusion at the end of each rowing season, and Tom's response to my cry was always the same, "You can do it. Don't give up now."

The difficulty of training for this sport was not only the dedication of hours of training, but also the long periods of time spent traveling and training abroad. My university education suffered, my new married life was not normal due to long absences from each other, and I had little social life. Tom made a supreme effort to visit me in training camps, but my focus was clearly on rowing and couldn't be divided. I recall the time Tom came to London, Ontario to see me during our winter training camp before we went to Florida and then on to Europe during the Olympic year. We wanted to stay together for a week or so, but the head national coach would not allow such privileges; it might distract me from rowing and tire me out. I was the only married athlete in the sculling camp, but I was treated like all the other athletes, with rigid bed times and afternoon rest between training workouts. My rowing partner, Bev Cameron, who was also my roommate, disappeared for a few evenings so I could spend some time with my husband, who had to sneak into the dormitory at night. We felt like a pair of bad kids. Only the athletes knew, I'm sure!

Tom was also in pursuit of his dream to wear a Canadian tracksuit and then to go on and compete in the Olympic marathon, a distance of 26 miles, 385 yards. Like many athletes, his reason for pursuit of excellence was for the personal satisfaction of bettering his performance, to see how fast he really could race.

His coach, Doug Clement, said Tom had great natural talent for running long distances. I remember the doctor telling Tom that his heart was much larger than a normal person, as proven by his resting pulse rate of 34 beats per minute. His stress level in training and racing was lower than any athlete I knew. He was never concerned about getting to a race or his start position on time, even when I was panicking over his last minute rituals, late arrival and slow pace to the start. He definitely had the making of a true marathoner's mind—low key, emotionally steady and seemingly impervious to pressure and pain.

I'll never forget the time Tom needed to prepare for a three-quarter marathon in Puerto Rico in 1973. Doug Clement had him ride a stationary bike in a sauna to acclimatize him to high humidity and heat. At that time Tom was a bus driver with a four-hour split shift in the middle of the day, so he always used his break to go on a twenty-mile training run.

Tom's training for the Olympics

In fact, Tom always managed to have some kind of a running commentary about his work, whether working as a 'postie' delivering mail house to house, or driving a city bus up and down Granville Street. There were times when he had to run away, mailbag and all, from pursuing dogs. He once had to or run away from an angry truck driver attacking with a metal pipe to take revenge on poor Tom, who had supposedly cut him off. Running always came in handy for Tom as it got him where he had to go!

My reasons for competing in rowing were many. I wanted to achieve something special and be a success in life. I also wanted to gain approval from my peers and praise from my parents. Most of all, I wanted to rise above the difficult years of feeling like a social misfit and not liking myself in my early youth. Whatever the reason, one thing was for sure— the sport of rowing had grown on me so much that I had begun to believe in that Olympic dream and take hold of it personally. I made a conscious decision to 'fight for it' all the way!

4.

Not Good Enough

*A*fter overcoming the many trials of the final training camp in Florida and fiercely fighting to hold on to my position in the double sculls boat while the team was continually downsizing, a straight path was made to my Olympic dream. Tom and I were both honored to be named to the 1976 Olympic Team, which was really special for us as a husband and wife couple. There were only two married couples on the entire Canadian Olympic team (Thelma Fynn and Lee Wright were the other couple). It was special that my parents and a few family members were there in Montreal to cheer and support us in the culmination of our many years of dedication and success. One image from my Olympic experience that stands out the most in my mind is that of the Canadian team entering last into the Montreal Olympic stadium to the deafening roar and applause of 60,000 people. I was so proud to represent my country and achieve a goal so few ambitious athletes reach.

My rowing partner, Bev Cameron, from Ottawa, and our Romanian coach, Anna Tomas, from Philadelphia, and myself were all poised for a good result in our double sculls event. Our first task was to do what no other women's sculling boat had accomplished—to qualify for the grand final race. We had to place first or second in the semi-finals to advance to the grand final. When we stormed down the Olympic basin to beat the French crew by a narrow margin of four hundredths of a second we knew history had been made in women's sculling.

Tom and I in Olympic Village, Montreal (1969)

But there was no energy to be lost in revelry, as we had to quickly refocus for the final race. A great crowd of spectators cheered Bev and I as we rowed up to the start of the final race. We were pitted against the top five crews in the world, most of them being Eastern European giants who most likely took some kind of drug to enhance their performance. We concentrated on only one thing, our race plan! Adrenalin was pumping wildly, yet each stroke had to be mastered in perfect precision and harmony. We had little race experience to our credit, but our heart and desire was to perform our best for Canada.

When the starter shouted, "Etes vous pres? Partez!" our racing shell surged into the 1000-meter race. Our lack of experience proved us no match for the highly competitive Europeans. We raced to a sixth place in the Olympic final. Based on Canadian sculling standards it was a good result! It should have been a great day of rejoicing and satisfaction, but deep down inside my partner, coach and myself knew that we had rowed below our potential; we weren't satisfied. We were hungry for a higher performance. We needed more international competition, which the Canadian Sporting Federation could not afford for rowers.

Olympic Double Sculls: Bev Cameron and I (1976)

On the last day of the Montreal Olympics, Tom competed in his race, the marathon! I am sure he lost some of his energy just waiting for his race and cheering for Bev and I at the beginning of the Olympics. Tom went into the Olympics with a standing of 13th best marathoner in the world. He had developed an achilles injury after being chosen for the Olympic team. This injury kept him training on a bicycle while his competitors pounded miles on the road. Tom bravely kept his mental state together

and focused on placing in the top ten, despite his
setback. I was in the Olympic stadium grandstand
watching the big screen when Tom came running
into the stadium and finally finished 30th. It was
over, but not the end for Tom as he went on to race
many more marathons, totaling 48 in all. Tom was
not a quitter even when sick, injured or fatigued. It
was always important to him to give his best effort
for the sake of his own conscience. I respected Tom's
ability to stay steady and focused no matter what the
challenge.

5.

The Agony and the Ecstasy

$\mathcal{B}$ev and I were a partnership that few understood. We were not powerful looking, stocky in build, tall, or even terribly experienced, but we were unified in the boat technically, mentally and physiologically. We were both committed to earning a medal in the next year's World Rowing Championships in Amsterdam, Holland. Bev relocated to Vancouver so we could train full time as a team in the double sculls boat. We also started the training year with a new coach, Stan Murza, from Ontario. Stan was a great coach for Bev and I as he worked with us to produce the harmony and precision necessary for success. Bev and I became close friends as we spent hours training on and off the water together, but as we drew nearer to that day of the Worlds in Amsterdam, something went terribly wrong.

Training for the 1977 World Rowing Championships in Amsterdam was full-time now since I had finally completed my Bachelor of Physical Education at the University of British Columbia. All coaches and top athletes know that when the highest level of fitness is achieved an athlete teeters on the border of fatigue and breakdown. An athlete can only reach and maintain his or her peak level of performance for a short period of time, and I was teetering on this fine edge while in Amsterdam. The National rowing coach, Tudor Bompa, and our coach started to see alarming signs: I had lost weight from 140 pounds to 120 pounds, fatigue was setting in and my inter-costal rib muscles were painfully sore. Our training quickly tapered off to nothing as my muscles screamed in pain. I tried to eat more carbohydrates to gain weight and my coach gave me the special privilege of drinking a beer a day to help put on weight. I also enjoyed eating a large milk chocolate bar after the day's workout. Nonetheless, the injured rib muscles kept me from even holding onto the oar grips. My partner and I were devastated. The specialists at a hospital in Amsterdam tried ultrasound treatment on my ribs, but to no avail. Painkillers were offered to me, but I knew that my future health was at stake and I was not willing to do anything risky that I would regret later.

It was at this time, while at the end of my resources, that I was most open to God's help and intervention. In my pursuit of God I began asking myself questions. Is God still there for me? Does He care about my dilemma? Has He forgotten me as I have Him? Is faith in God real? I began to pray earnestly for God to reveal Himself and His will to me at that time. Great pressure was being applied to me as I complained of not being able to row. My partner trained with the sculling spare on the team, who happened to be her sister, Trice Cameron. I sought God with all my heart and I came to realize that God did not just want a part time relationship with me whenever I was in trouble. He wanted me to trust Him for all of my life, good or bad. Under great pressure people have made deals with God to get them out of a bind. Time was running out and I was in a bind.

What was I to do? I couldn't row in excruciating pain. Everyone expected us to at least get a bronze medal—we were fine-tuned for performing our best. Was God even interested in my rowing career at this most tenuous moment of my life? While listening in my heart to the only One who could help me I sensed a determination to row and trust Him. I was prepared for something unusual, a divine intervention. I didn't want to make a deal with God. I only wanted a sign that He cared about my life.

In the first rowing race or heat, it was agreed that I would sit in the usual stroke seat in the stern of the boat, but I would not actively row. I would only balance the boat, as Bev would take us to the finish line in our heat. The double sculls event was always a very popular and highly competitive entry at the Worlds and so there were many boats competing to make the Final. This strategy of me not rowing in the boat kept us still in the race, leaving opportunity for something to happen in the next qualifying round, the repechage. Every crew had a second chance to qualify if they rowed the first heat. I felt foolish not rowing, but strangely confident in God for the first time.

The second rowing race, the repechage, was the 'cruncher' where we had to place first or second to advance to the Grand Final. It was all or nothing! It was a great risk of integrity and honor when I decided to row regardless of the pain. My partner was greatly relieved and confident, despite our loss of training time together. I knew that I could do nothing unless God provided a way. Today, I still remember our start. It was smooth and perfect! There was no pain! We rowed the perfect race and managed to hang on to battle for second. We crossed the finish line in a blur with Russia. It was a photo finish as both balls of the boats were inseparable on the electronic photo.

World Championships in Amsterdam (1977)
Bev and I qualify for the Final—Agony and Ecstasy!

We waited in agony for the results to flash up on the overhead screen. It was amazing! We defeated Russia by 4/100ths of a second! The ecstasy was ours! My partner grabbed my shirt and yelled, "We made it!" as I was bent over holding my head in preparation for defeat. We rejoiced together. We had defeated a crew that probably depended on drugs and other aids to perform at the top world level. Russia had never been knocked out of a final and they were furious! The Russian team was not going to row the petite final (the consolation race) until the FISA Rowing Committee warned them that the entire Russian team would be sent home if they were poor sports by not rowing in the consolation race. And so, in humiliation, they stayed to finish competing in the consolation round.

Was the agony really over? There was one more race to row, the Grand Final. We still had a chance to win a medal at the Worlds! My fitness and adrenalin were high even though I hadn't rowed properly in weeks. I felt that my coach, fellow athletes and rowing partner were all in denial that I had had a true injury after they witnessed my comeback. I am sure they wondered how it was possible for me to row if my muscles were damaged. I tried to explain to my coach, partner and other rowing comrades that I had prayed and trusted God, but only one friend, Joy Fera, actually listened and believed my testimony.

There was little recovery time as we had to row again in the next few days. I felt confident to risk trusting God again as I felt that He had a plan for me. Little did I know that the Grand Final of the World Rowing Championships would later become the hallmark of my rowing career, really connecting me to God! Our start was explosive at 45 strokes per minute! Again there was no pain! The stroke rate was too high for our fitness as we went off in great gusto and confidence. At the halfway point we 'hit the wall' of lactic acid overload and fell from second place to third, and then just barely hanging on to a fourth place finish. As the stroke person in the stern of the boat, it was my responsibility to set the pace and rhythm for the entire race as practiced and planned ahead. Again, race experience was our greatest weakness, as I lost focus on the race pace at the very beginning. A perfect race means peaking on race day and staying completely focused on the race plan. Would we ever get another opportunity for medals?

No one could have predicted the outcome for Bev and I at the World Rowing Championships in Amsterdam. Everyone was devastated for us that we did not gain the medal we had set our hopes on for that year, but in reality, there was something greater than my disappointment; it was experiencing God's grace. He had allowed me to row, despite the odds against me. The outcome of the race was our responsibility, not God's. He took away the injury and pain so I could row. When I think of the little attention and honor I had given God in the past, I was so undeserving of His grace. I truly wanted to discover more of His grace for my life.

Tom encouraged me to keep striving for the top. We had both made sacrifices for one another's sporting careers and I couldn't quit now. Bev and I realized our true potential as world-class scullers and recommitted to yet another year of training hard together. How would my rowing career end?

6.

God Speaks!

Tom and I training together in 1978

Any married athlete will tell you that marriage is hard enough to keep healthy, let alone when put on hold while you are pursuing your personal dreams and goals. My heart and desire was to remain in rowing one more year, so Tom encouraged me to go to Australia for training and competition and then on to New Zealand for the World Rowing Championships. He had planned to meet me in Australia and race a marathon in New Zealand he was invited to. It was certainly a year that I needed his emotional support.

Bev and I rowed to an easy win in the National doubles event. We were excited about our potential for medals in the Worlds. However, our hopes were quickly dashed when my rowing partner, Bev, did not make the National team in the double with me and this was a great upset for us. We had trained very hard in the double at Burnaby Lake under a British coach to prepare for a medal at the Worlds, but for some unexpected reason, the head rowing coach made us race in singles to prove our individual fitness before being named to the Canadian team. Since Bev and I had not trained in singles all year we were not in top form for singles racing and thus we both did not perform according to our ability. Racing in singles requires a different feel than the double and we were not prepared for this sudden switch.

In our opinion the selection process was unfair. It meant Bev had to go, since she did not place in the top two positions in the deciding singles' race. We were both extremely devastated over the loss of our dreams and partnership and we doubted that we would ever row again together as we parted in frustration and hurt. We tried to convince the National Rowing Committee to reconsider their decision, but to no avail.

My new partner and I began training with her coach. My heart was still with Bev, because I yearned for that unique harmony we had gained through miles and miles of rowing together. My new partner and I never had the time to mesh technically or psychologically before we arrived at the Worlds, plus I was sick in Australia so we missed our only international competition to sharpen us for the Worlds. In New Zealand on Lake Karapiro, the weather condition for our rowing heat was so severe that rowing was postponed one day. Eventually, we had to row, regardless of the unfair racing conditions. As we floundered in rough waves and adverse wind conditions to the finish line we did no better than qualifying for the Petite Finals. It was a great disappointment for both of us not to make the Grand Finals in the double sculls event. Even so, I breathed a long awaited sigh of relief when our rowing was finished.

World Rowing Championship, New Zealand (1978)
Andrea Schreiner and I in the Repachage
(heat for final qualification)

Thankfully, my last year of rowing represented something far more important than performance or winning medals. I wanted to honor God for endowing me with athletic talent, which had helped me reach fourth best in the Worlds and given me so many traveling opportunities. I remember specifically praying that God would allow me to do something for Him.

The idea came to me to give a Bible to a Russian athlete, which was not really allowed. At that time Russia was a communist country and especially closed to Christian influence. I remember reading a book by Brother Andrew, called *God's Smuggler*. His life was spent smuggling Bibles into Russia because there was such a cry for God's Word in this love-starved nation. My heartfelt goal was to place a Russian Bible into the hands of a young rower who desired it and knew of its worth. When I arrived in New Zealand I remembered asking someone if there was a Christian bookstore nearby. We were not living close to town and I expected to have to travel some distance to find one. As it happened, there was a Christian bookstore just a short walk from our motel, down the country road. It was quite an unusual place for a bookstore, I thought.

I went quickly and inquired about a Russian Bible. Oddly enough, they had ordered Bibles in different languages because of the world-rowing event. I was amazed as they handed me the only remaining Russian Bible. What an encouragement to me. During the final week of competition at Lake Karapiro I tried to make friends with a young Russian girl who spoke English. She rowed in a coxed four crew. Near the end of the week I gained enough courage to ask her if she would accept a Russian Bible. Our relationship was over as she flatly refused and walked away in haste. I could certainly understand her fear of being caught with a Bible.

World Rowing Championship, New Zealand (1978)
Russian athlete who would not take a Bible

On the last day of rowing competition I had become quite frantic about giving the Bible to the right person. Not many Russians spoke English and they kept to themselves. The problem was solved in an unusual way when a woman called to me out of a crowd of spectators.

World Rowing Championship, New Zealand (1978)
Last day crowd of spectators

"Excuse me. Are you Cheryl?"

"Yes," I responded with curiosity.

"I was told that a Canadian athlete named Cheryl had a Russian Bible," she explained.

"How did you get that information?" I asked in amazement.

"The Christian bookstore sold you their only Russian Bible and I wanted to give one to an athlete. The store owner gave me a description of you and I've been searching for you every day." She added, "The Lord told me the name of the athlete you should give this Bible to. His name is Vladimir."

Wow, we were both stunned! What an amazing God to get this vital information to me through a complete stranger. I realized that there really must be someone who wants this precious book. Now my mission was almost complete, but where was this rower? Anticipation and excitement welled up in my heart as I thought about what to do. Time was running out, so I promptly took the wrapped package and proceeded to search for Vladimir.

Thousands of spectators and athletes were milling around during the final hours of the last day. I began walking in the direction of crews working on their boats. I spotted a crew of Russians working on their rowing shell. In a friendly and calm manner I walked up to a Russian male rower and asked him if he spoke English.

He responded, "Yes".

I asked further, "Is there someone on your team with the name Vladimir?"

He answered, "Yes," again, and pointed me in the direction of a Russian crew going out to row a race.

It was thrilling to watch this crew race to a gold medal. While waiting in anticipation of the crew's arrival, an idea quickly came. I approached another Russian rower who was working on his boat, and asked him which athlete in the crew was Vladimir. I explained that I had a gift for him for winning the gold medal and asked him if he would translate for me if Vladimir couldn't understand English. He walked up to Vladimir and brought him to me. I congratulated Vladimir on his gold medal win with his crew and told him that God had a special gift for him, more valuable than his gold medal and asked him if he would accept a Russian Bible. He immediately said, "Yes," and with enthusiasm and a smile he received the package. It was obvious that he was very thankful. It was a thrilling moment that had to end quickly before anyone became suspicious of our actions.

It was thrilling for me to see him receive this gift and know that I had really heard from God. All my training to come to New Zealand and the disappointment of rowing far below expectation was worth the experience of giving the Russian rower something precious from God. This rewarding experience was indelibly imprinted in my memory. It brought a culmination to a season of my life. It was a sovereign orchestration of God that spurred me on to change my heart towards God and care about people. Even though I loved the sport of rowing, my heart and desire was no longer to push myself to the limits required in elite competition. I was ready to refocus!

7.

Nothing New!

*A*fter my rowing career came to a direct halt my husband and I were ready to start our family. Francine arrived on the scene in December 1979. She stole our hearts and comforted me from the loss of my rowing career. During the next six years we went on to have two more children, Courtney and Andrew. We were busy parents of three, but during those fun years of raising toddlers and home schooling, Tom and I found time to start a road running club in south Surrey, the Semiahmoo Sunrunners, which is still thriving today.

It seemed that the adrenalin for competitive sports was still strong in me. I loved the sense of purpose it brought to my life, being someone who was always seeking a new challenge and desiring to learn new things. While raising our three children Tom continued with his marathon running and I found new sports to challenge my fitness and abilities. I competed in three cross-country ski races, one being the B.C. Winter Games for masters in Fort Saint John and the other two were the Caribou ski marathon. I did some rowing on a lower level for fun and began to train for long distance races since my body was so fit from the past four years of rowing training.

A special achievement in my athletic career (which my husband talked me into) was training and eventually racing a marathon. After watching Tom train and race marathons for several years I was very intrigued as to whether or not I could actually race and complete the marathon distance. However, there was the cost to consider of training long, lonely miles and many discomforts to racing 26 miles. There is little glamour to the sport of marathon racing because of the many obstacles and hardships, such as rashes between the legs, blistered feet, loss of toenails, muscular cramping near and after the finish, hitting the physiological wall and a sick stomach from dehydration. I had seen Tom experience all these ill effects, but maybe my experience would be more sane and delightful!

A running friend, Debbie, helped me put in some long slow runs of twelve miles as well as one twenty-miler. In six months of comfortable training (sometimes while pushing the stroller with our firstborn) I was ready for race day at the National marathon in Vancouver.

God definitely was a huge factor in that race. During the first fifteen kilometers of the marathon around Stanley Park I was running with an older gentleman, Stan Baldry. I shared with him my huge struggle with a severe stitch (cramps) that had started at the beginning of the race. My pace was about six minutes, thirty seconds a mile and I knew I would run a fair time if I kept going, but my stomach pains were a great deterrent. Stan heard my prayer as I called out to God for healing and mercy to be able to finish the race. Within a short distance around Gas Town my stomach cramps completely disappeared, something I had never experienced before in racing.

With eleven miles left I had a great surge of adrenalin and said goodbye to Stan as I sped up to finish the race with increased strength. After climbing the last hill the finish banner loomed ahead and I was under it in two hours and fifty-eight minutes. I did not expect to finish fourth Canadian and in a time under three hours! I was so thankful to God for saving me a second time in my racing career. Needless to say, I was very stiff and sore immediately after crossing the finish line. I learned to go down stairs backwards and to keep moving slowly. That was my one and only marathon; enough experience to appreciate my husband's talent in enduring pain and pounding miles on the road by himself. The life of a lonely distance runner was not my forte!

One of the most interesting sports I pursued for two years was the modern pentathlon, which included, shooting, horse jumping, cross country running, swimming and fencing. I placed well in the Nationals, coming fourth, but did not continue to train as I felt beyond my years for beginning such a demanding sport.

National Championship in the Modern Pentathalon (1 of 5 events) Stadium jumping on 'Mo'

Another new sport I had been dreaming about brought me back to my passion for horses. I had a horse crazy moment when I decided to buy an Egyptian Arab, Genti, for the purpose of racing long distances of up to one hundred miles. This Arab, out of the bloodline of El Hilal, had great potential and so we started putting in our miles. I was very naïve about horses and never considered the fact that a green (newly broken) three-year old horse was a very good cause for caution and correct training. In retrospect, my 'self' still needed to identify with performance as I rebounded from one sport to another, never fully satisfied, always trying to fill a need. Would I ever reach that place of fulfillment in my life?

8.

Lights Out!

*I*t was another grand day for a ride with some of my horsy friends. Genti, my athletic gray mare, and I were becoming good partners and I loved to ride her whenever possible. This day's ride was different from all other rides because there was a novice rider accompanying myself and another experienced rider.

Genti, my Arab mare

When we arrived at a riding ring a few miles from home, the novice rider's mount took off towards home, thinking this was the turn around point. My other friend didn't notice what was happening and proceeded to gallop her horse over a jump in the ring. Genti was a very sensitive and alert horse and so she reacted with excitement by wanting to surge after the runaway horse. My first response was to hold her back from being a second runaway horse out of control, but before I could think further, Genti reared up in defiance and together we toppled over backwards. She didn't land on top of me, but there was a sharp pain in my spine as I hit the ground hard. When I got up to get back on my horse, my head and neck cried out that something was terribly wrong.

For the next two years my body was in a state of trauma as I tried various chiropractic treatments, not even thinking of going to my regular doctor. My children and husband looked after me through the many migraine headaches and spasms that were common throughout my recovery. Eventually, I accepted the fact that it would take several years for my body to find comfort and strength. I decided to stop getting further chiropractic treatment because I was continually dependent on adjustments for relief of pain, and I was afraid of co-dependency. In the meantime, I was forced to stop all work and ambitious endeavors in sports or otherwise.

I remember this time as if the lights in my life were turned out. It was a dark, scary and lonely battle of pain and trauma. It was a time of stillness for my soul to meditate on much of my life and God's will for me. Over time, with much prayer, encouragement and ministry from friends, I received great inner healing from God and new hope sprung forth. Where was my heart and desire now? It was no longer in pursuit of success, identity and performance, which had occupied me for years; it was in pursuit of something much higher and deeper! But what was that? Like a baton being passed into a runner's hand, I sensed that an exchange was coming into my life, one that would have eternal value.

9.

Into Deeper Waters

*S*hortly after this serious physical setback in my life we took up the challenge to move to Maple Ridge and help start a new church along with some other couples. We were moving away from familiarity, comfort and friends, but we were also stepping out in faith that God had something new for our family. Tom continued to drive busses out of another station and I pursued home schooling and Sunday School teaching. For two and a half years we thoroughly enjoyed the challenge of a new life in the Whonnock community where we were involved with horses and people in a most pleasurable way.

Restlessness came over us and we again sought to move to a less busy place where life would continue to offer much to our three adventuresome and athletic children. We sought out many recreational communities and through a series of confirmations we knew we should move to the Comox Valley where I had been born and where my mother had just moved to retire.

I still remember the moving day as we loaded up the back of Tom's pick-up truck for the first trip to the Island. The long wait at the Horseshoe Bay ferry was endured on the hottest day that summer and our animals were feeling the heat. Fortunately, we happened to park in the line right under an overhang near the ferry ramp. What a relief it was to have shade that day! The next moving day for Tom was like running two marathons back-to-back. He was so exhausted and stressed that I came to realize how much my husband sacrificed for our love of animals and adventure. We moved our four horses, two goats, two dogs and two cats to live with us on our beautiful forty-acre farm and wonderful farmhouse with a wraparound deck.

I am sure that God handpicked this place for us, because we ended up living there eleven years, many years longer than in any other home. Not long after we arrived to our new homestead, my favorite Appaloosa mare, Honey Bumble Bee, had a foal, Rocky Bee Sweet (Rocky). This foal was going to be my horse while growing old, so I could ride off into the sunset!

Foal, 'Rocky Bee Sweet' (1992)

10.

Accidents Do Happen

I am glad that we don't always know what is up ahead for us in life. This was particularly true one afternoon in the spring of 2001, when my riding friend Margaret and I went for our usual weekly ride. Two of my children were home on our country acreage that eventful day. Fourteen-year old Andrew was practicing his golf shots on the front lawn and Grace, our six-year old daughter, was happily watching her brother. It was a perfect day for a leisurely ride, especially on my seven-year old gelding, Rocky. I had not ridden him enough to really feel relaxed in the saddle, as he always seemed to intimidate me by his over sixteen hands height and challenging attitude. He was just that kind of a horse that you had to feel 'up' to ride.

Looking back on that day is difficult for me, as all I can remember are brief flashes of surprise, panic, terror and relief. Surprise, because Rocky, seemingly unprovoked, catapulted forward and up into the air after only taking a few steps. This happened before my hands had sufficiently collected the reins and my feet had found their resting-place in the stirrups. Rocky had not hinted of any saddling anxiety until that terrifying moment when his prey instinct reacted to some unknown monster. Panic took hold of me, because I knew I could not control his wild and powerful crow hops as his stiff body and legs sprung straight up in the air like a pogo stick.

Each of his four crow hops sent me flying into a different position on his body, over his neck and behind the saddle, which greatly added to his agitation. And finally, terror hit as I was bounced into the air, only to come crashing down on my back and land on the gravel driveway. Unfortunately, not all of me hit the ground, because my legs stayed suspended in the air, caught by the reins. I gave a big kick and tug with my legs to set them free just as Rocky's powerful frame loomed over me with another crow hop. His feet lightly brushed my body as I agonizingly rolled onto my stomach. Ugh!

Even though I had broken free from Rocky's perilous antics I was not able to breathe or move. The sudden impact left my body in painful spasms. My riding partner quickly restrained her mount to a tie ring and ran over to inspect my condition. (Rocky had gone off crow hopping and soon returned to a sullen position not far away.) After Margaret and Andrew tried moving me unsuccessfully to a sitting position, Andrew ran into the house to call 911 and to contact my prayer partner for help.

"Mom are you going to die?" was Grace's first remark. Soon the ambulance came and I was carried away, lying flat out on a hard stretcher board. After a seemingly long wait, the x-rays showed no broken bones, just a lot of bad bruises, sore bones and pulled muscles. My family helped me hobble out of the hospital not knowing that Rocky and I were traumatized forever, and that we would eventually embark on a life-changing journey—'the better way.'

Riding partners: Marg Suther on 'Chilko,' Betty Parlee on 'Prince' and me on 'Rocky'

11.

A Major Setback

*M*ost everyone has suffered emotional trauma in varying degrees. An extreme example I well remember reading in the newspaper (and later in a book) was of a woman's near death encounter with a grizzly bear, which left her with a lifelong battle for recovery. Such emotional and physical scarring can sometimes be a constant nightmare until one day there comes a ray of hope, a breakthrough, a point of moving on in the healing process. The battle to recover from emotional and physical trauma is always worthwhile when you look back and realize that you are no longer a victim but a victor!

Over the past twenty-five years our family has owned over twenty-four horses. My riding experiences have been varied and challenging, but never has my emotional fitness been undermined as it was with this one particular horse, Rocky. Rocky was born nine years ago from our Appaloosa mare, Honey Bumble Bee. The sire was a Tennessee Walker, Sun's Rocky Velvet, owned by the Smith's at Tower Ridge Farms. Rocky was a new breed of horse called a Walkaloosa, supposedly a spotted walking horse.

My troubles with Rocky started way back when his second trainer was professionally training him. Rocky did not take kindly to being girthed up tightly when he hadn't had a saddle on his back for months.

Consequently the trainer was bucked off twice in a row, leaving her with a bleeding nose and a wounded ego. I quickly suggested that we begin on the ground first and then approach riding when she got to know Rocky better. Unfortunately, Rocky never recovered from that very traumatic event of tight girthing. Whether or not he had a physical excuse or simply a fear of girths, we only knew for sure that Rocky needed lots of retraining.

After much ring work with the trainer, Rocky and I were able to get started on the road and trails. Over time Rocky developed sensitivity to the girth again. It was so extreme that every time I saddled Rocky he would take off like a balloon losing air, crow hopping all over the property. It was not a pretty sight. Every time he went through this bucking routine I was gripped with fear and trepidation. There came a point that I could not saddle him unless I had help, but I was always able to ride Rocky after he finished his bucking bout, until that one surprising and traumatic day when he got the better of me. It became very clear to me that I needed to make a very difficult decision of what to do with Rocky and my choices were very limited.

12.

Challenge or Defeat!

*C*an you remember a time when you were faced with a challenge, whether it was physical, emotional or mental? What made the difference between giving up and forging ahead? For me, what made the difference between quitting and persisting was a choice I made to trust God for a faint ray of hope, which came in the form of encouragement. Horses are not worth risking your life for, so I realized that if I was to work through my emotional trauma and find answers for Rocky, it had to be relatively safe for me. It had to be a totally new approach compared to what I was doing. I must mention here that I did pray and wait for an answer from God before making a decision. I wanted to do the right thing and have God's permission and provision from start to finish.

The encouragement came through a strange series of events. A neighbor's lonely horse, Avalon, came into our yard one evening and later the owner came to fetch her back for the umpteenth time. She knew of my dilemma with Rocky and asked how I was doing with him. When I told her I had exhausted every avenue I knew about, she mentioned her success with Avalon. My first glimmer of hope came as I listened to her explain the huge transformation that she and her horse had encountered through a new style of training called 'natural horsemanship,' under the instruction of a trainer, Susan Warner.

Her horse certainly was different in his behavior and countenance. I was impressed with the little demonstration she gave me as she hopped onto her horse bareback. Using only a light halter and lead rope on one side, rather than reins, she rode home at a quiet pace. A few days later, after much deliberation, I phoned Susan Warner and asked for her help. She easily agreed to come and assess my situation with Rocky. I was greatly encouraged by her sympathetic heart and keenness to help.

Susan Warner on 'Mirage'

13.

Help Comes in the
Form of Grace

I'll always remember the first day Susan met Rocky. It was in a little makeshift round pen that she had asked me to prepare ahead of their arrival. I could not imagine what their first meeting would be like, because I knew nothing about Susan's training methods. Rocky did not know it was his trial, to discover whether he was dangerous or trainable. During that first extraordinary encounter, I witnessed strange and dynamic principles I had never heard of—Natural Horsemanship.

Application of Natural Horsemanship Principles in My Life

At the same time that Rocky and I were undergoing a change in relationship, I happened to be studying the first eight chapters of the Biblical book of Romans with a large group of friends who came to our home every week. I began to see a parallel between Natural Horsemanship and God's message of 'grace,' as taught by the Apostle Paul in the book of Romans. It was truly an astounding and exciting revelation. God knew how to captivate my heart through my horse.

Natural Horsemanship and God's grace are both about a powerful, loving relationship built through a bond of trust and respect. A gentle and patient 'leader,' who asks for a willing partner, initiates this relationship. There is freedom to choose either to go or to stay and find comfort and fulfillment. Rocky and I were gradually changed by this wonderful grace experience, which I realized was really a picture of who Jesus is to me, the Lover of my soul.

Biblical Application

II Samuel 22:36

King David spoke these words while praising God in song: *"...Your gentleness has made me great."*

II Peter 3:18

"...but grow in the grace and knowledge of our Lord and Savior Jesus Christ."

14.

∽∞∽

The Battle Against Grace

*B*efore Susan worked with Rocky she explained to me how horses think and act. I learned that horses are naturally prey animals with an innate sense of 'fright and flight' for preservation from predators. Horses actually view people as predators, or meat eaters, an interesting fact that I never knew. The best way to change that prey-predator relationship is to work with the horse using its own language, called 'equs.' Most horse owners don't realize that when they are just hanging out with their horse by grooming it, stroking it and playing with it, a natural bonding is happening, a part of 'equs,' or horse talk. Equs is learned by observing horses in their natural state with a herd, where there is a stallion running with his mares and their foals. The stallion will dominate the mares by using his body language and energy. He is the 'alpha' or lead horse and all other horses follow him. I certainly liked the idea of being the 'leader' and Rocky not being fearful and running away.

Susan further explained some basic principles of natural horsemanship training. She said that the first phase of naturally training a horse is called 'join up.' The horse learns that you are the alpha—the leader and his comfort. The horse will willingly come to you when called. There is no pain inflicted, only the mildest form of restraint, if necessary. It's never,

"You must!" but always, "Here's your opportunity, now take it." Pressure always brings flight, so using a technique of 'advance and retreat' where the horse is free and not restricted is the best non-threatening approach to building a relationship. This wonderful concept of Rocky coming to me of his own free will was something I had to see before believing. The thought of letting Rocky go free and winning his heart and desire was quite a challenge to my way of working with horses. I always felt that horses were more interested in grass and each other than hanging out with people and that it was always the halter and lead rope, or bridle and bit that made a horse pay attention to its master. I began to feel like I knew very little about horses even after spending twenty-five years with them. Susan challenged me to trust her and not get frustrated or impatient with Rocky's progress.

Application of Natural Horsemanship Principles in My Life

I found out that being a recipient of God's grace means precisely that, letting go of all my expectations and letting God lead the way. Giving up 'old ways' of doing things and being open to learning new ways certainly was difficult. True humility started to form in my being, where I was becoming a learner again instead of a 'know-it-all.' I started to see how resistant I really was to letting God lead and trusting in His ways. Being in control and leading were natural for me from childhood, because I loved to be bossy and play the role of 'teacher.' However, I wanted to grow in God's grace and experience a greater love relationship with Him, so I gradually began the process of listening, cooperating and 'letting go...' for something better!

Biblical Application

Proverbs 3:5-6

"Trust in the Lord with all your heart, and lean not on your own understanding; in all your ways acknowledge Him, and He shall direct your paths."

James 4:6

"God resists the proud, but gives grace to the humble."

15.

The Join Up

$\mathcal{T}$he 'join up' first began in the makeshift round pen where Rocky was freely running around the perimeter while avoiding Susan who was standing in the middle with her long rope. Amazingly, after a long period of time, and just as Susan had predicted, Rocky cocked an ear, began blinking and turned his head toward her, showing signs of yielding and respect. As soon as she moved backward while not looking at Rocky to give him comfort, he would dash off like a frightened prey animal because he was confused and still not trusting. Susan made the choice very clear to Rocky. He would find comfort when he came in to her or he would find work on the outside of the ring when he wanted to remain resistant and independent to her invitation.

Eventually it happened. Rocky stopped, turned, and curiously stepped toward Susan to investigate her non-threatening actions as she slowly backed away a little, giving an invitation to come, and further beckoned him in with her hand and body language. It was all so wonderful and incredible as this big, steaming black horse focused on Susan and cautiously walked directly toward her with his head high and body alert for flight. He stood facing Susan like a soldier saluting his captain. He sighed to let out stress and slowly began chewing, which is a sign of thinking about what just happened. In an instant, at Susan's slightest movement to stroke Rocky with the coiled rope, he turned and fled. The rope was his enemy when it came into his personal space. This game of advance and retreat continued until Rocky was thoroughly convinced that Susan and the rope were friendly and meant no harm.

The whole scene was like watching a lover woo his love with great patience, gentleness and encouragement. Each time Rocky was called in by Susan he stayed with her longer and longer, until he realized she was 'safe' and his 'comfort.' In the end, Rocky made his choice and they walked off freely together as partners around the ring. Rocky showed respect by not turning his rump to Susan and he kept his head low by her shoulder as he followed whichever way she turned. I was greatly impressed with Susan's sensitivity and unique ability to predict Rocky's actions. At the end of two and a half hours Rocky had softened dramatically and to my surprise and delight he had 'joined-up' with Susan of his own free will. Now with the 'join-up' complete their partnership could go forward.

After a few sessions with Rocky, Susan announced that he was an intelligent and sensitive horse. She was willing to work with Rocky and me if I was willing to trust her judgment and wait for the results. She assessed that Rocky was a domineering gelding who wanted to be boss. He was operating out of fear instead of understanding and trust. I definitely should not have been riding Rocky under those conditions. Susan could see that my emotional fitness was very damaged from two years of Rocky's bucking sessions and from my serious fall. I needed to learn to trust him all over again. Horses never respond positively towards methods of force, manipulation, fear or intimidation, so we had to build new foundations of trust and respect to win his heart and desire.

First round pen work: Rocky and I in the beginning stages of learning Natural Horsemanship

Application of Natural Horsemanship Principles in My Life

'Join-up with Rocky' was very similar to my own 'join up' with God when I was twelve years old. I was definitely a very independent, stubborn and self-willed child in my elementary years at school. It seemed that I had a reputation for being a troublemaker in my neighborhood and couldn't be trusted. I did not respect authority or have good relationships with most people.

My Nana influenced my parents in making us four children go to Sunday School. It was a long walk to get to Sunday School and it was a long wait before church was out, so I wasn't much interested in church until I met a special Sunday School teacher who sat her class at a round table to study Bible stories and plan a Christmas pageant. I was given the part of an angel dressed in a gown with a halo. Now that was encouraging to me!

Our neighbors across the street invited children over to participate in a Bible hour one day a week. They were a kind family, always letting the neighborhood children play games on their paved driveway. Years later, I found out that they prayed regularly for our family.

My oldest sister often shared her faith in God with me and encouraged me to trust God and to pray. Many times when I had been really bad and disobedient I felt guilt and shame and would lie on my bed telling God I was sorry and that I wouldn't do it again. Of course I was not strong enough to resist doing my own thing, so I always succumbed to temptation, but God was often on my mind, as I wanted to be obedient and pleasing to Him. During most of my childhood I felt alone, lonely and disconnected from most of reality. I watched hours of television, played with Barbie dolls and daydreamed in school. This continued until I had a spiritual breakthrough.

While in grade seven I was asked to accompany a classmate to Timberline Ranch for a summer camp. Never had I dreamed I could go to a ranch camp! All the girls that were asked declined, but I had permission to go because her parents were willing to pay my camp fee. The Christian camp offered many fun and challenging outdoor activities, such as horse riding, shooting and archery. As a child, it was my only opportunity to go to camp.

Every evening at campfire I heard the gospel message of Jesus Christ. On the final evening I felt near to God, and my heart was ready to make the greatest decision of my life. I knew I was a sinner and needed forgiveness to inherit eternal life with God. When the campfire time was over a female camp counselor came alongside me on a log near the campfire and asked if I wanted to invite Jesus into my heart. I was so nervous as my heart pounded loudly and my whole being was alert to the question. I said, "Yes," and so we prayed together in the dark and I asked Jesus to come into my heart and be my Lord and Savior. As I walked alone back to my cabin I knew that I was changed forever because my sin problem had been dealt with. I had no more guilt, shame and sorrow over my past and I had assurance that God had forgiven me and accepted me as His child.

In the past, I had judged God as distant, angry and harsh. I feared God in a negative way because of my bad relationship with both my birth father and stepfather. I never knew love and acceptance from either of them, so I could not easily understand my heavenly Father's unconditional love for me. God had been drawing me steadily closer over the years to show me His gentleness and tender love. My heart had become more and more aware and open to Him. Did I really know God? No, but He gave me a small measure of faith and grace to allow me to stop going my own way and turn to Him for salvation, comfort and guidance. I wanted peace in my heart and a true friend that I could depend upon. My life was very lonely and troubled so I was ready for a Friend—One who was all-seeing and all-understanding—a Friend to whom I could tell my woes and troubles just as they were.

Interestingly, as I look back now, I can see that God moved quickly after my salvation experience to bring a new direction into my life and to rescue me from many bad influences. He made it possible for me to join the local track club, as previously mentioned, because we moved closer to Minoru Park where I became focused on more healthy pursuits and had good role modeling from my running friends who encouraged and affirmed me.

'Join up' with God was the first step of faith in my relationship with God that would later require much more learning and cooperation with Him as the Alpha to really develop a harmonious relationship where I would give Him my heart and desire more and more. I was on a journey to discover God as my Father and thus find my own true identity.

Biblical Application

Matthew 11:28-30
"Come to Me, all you who labor and are heavy laden, and I will give you rest. Take My yoke upon you and learn from Me, for I am gentle and lowly in heart, and you will find rest for your souls. For My yoke is easy, and My burden is light."

II Corinthians 5:17
"Therefore, if anyone is in Christ, he is a new creation; old things have passed away; behold, all things have become new."

16.

The Friendly Game

*A*chieving the 'join-up' with Rocky was only the beginning of a long transformation that needed to take place in his mind, will and emotions. Rocky had a strong fear and flight instinct for self-preservation. In addition to this innate fear, Rocky seemed to have a much greater dose of independence than most horses, thus a bad attitude! Susan and I could only guess that he had been traumatized at some point in his early training, or that an accident unknown to us had caused him to put a big wall around himself to keep people out and not trust anyone. I couldn't accept the fact that Rocky would always be so intimidating to me and everyone else. He was my dream horse for pleasure riding and years of enjoyment. It certainly appeared to me that Natural Horsemanship was the right direction to pursue.

One of the great advantages of Natural Horsemanship training is that the horse learns to take on a new nature as it gives up its old nature of fear, flight and self-preservation in order to form a partnership of trust and respect. The prey-predator barrier has to be broken down. I definitely trusted Susan to guide me through this transformation process with Rocky. During this process I discovered that my own emotional fitness was also in dire need of healing and restoration, as my nerves were very shaky around Rocky. Natural Horsemanship principles were good for both of us.

The 'friendly game' was the first and most important game introduced to Rocky after the 'join-up.' This game helps to build a quality relationship where the leader gains the horse's confidence, acceptance and understanding. Always asking permission to enter the horse's personal space instead of forcing your way in shows consideration in your relationship. A twelve-foot rope is attached to a sensitive rope halter on the horse and is held loose and long, allowing the horse freedom to move away when uncomfortable. Body language communicates much of your heart to the horse about what you feel and want. A horse relaxes when its partner's body energy is low and non-threatening, and it becomes alert and perky when the person's energy comes up.

To prove to Rocky that I could be friendly and trusted I started rubbing Rocky all over his body with my hands in a rhythmical and friendly fashion, finding out where all his 'ya-but' and vulnerable areas were. Rocky loved being scratched and rubbed in certain areas, which produced a calming effect. For a while I would focus on these areas and then move to his head, a most sensitive area! Whenever Rocky communicated fear, distrust or any defensive reactions, I would not make an issue. Rather, I would respond politely by retreating and then advancing again more slowly using rhythm, gradually desensitizing Rocky. Punishment does not work with a prey animal, as it only causes more rebellion and hardness.

Gradually, we moved on to ask more from Rocky's emotional fitness. We introduced blankets, ropes and a carrot stick (a long orange stick with a thin string dangling off the end) by touching him all over with them. Slowly these items became a comfort to him. An example of a higher level of the 'friendly game' that took Rocky some time to accept was when

Susan used the progressive string on the end of the carrot stick to swing like a helicopter over his head, or wrap it around his legs, or when she slapped it furiously on the ground all around him and then suddenly lifted the string over his back to rub him gently. Rocky often tried to avoid the touching by jumping sideways, or spinning around, but Susan demonstrated great persistence, patience and gentleness toward Rocky, until she got a 'try' or a yield from him, which sometimes took many sessions of being 'friendly.' There are higher levels of trust that can be won over a lifetime through playing the 'friendly game'.

The traditional way of training a horse to accept scary things and obey is called 'sacking out' or 'breaking in.' The horse is made to stand by using mechanical means, and often tactics of intimidation and force are employed to frighten the horse into submission. It is a form of control by punishment, and is a very scary method for a horse to endure. In the end, the horse submits to the person, not out of willing cooperation, but out of fear. If this horse were given its freedom it would most likely run away or show aggression toward the person by rearing, bucking, kicking, biting or charging. It is obvious when you observe how horses respond to Natural Horsemanship techniques that they were created to be in harmony with people.

Even greater tests of Rocky's emotional fitness and our partnership would come later when he would be asked to cooperate in the 'friendly game' at liberty, without a halter, lead rope or a small ring to contain him. Our goal was to progress ahead in these areas so we could have many safe and happy trails together.

Friendly Game at Liberty, 'Helicopter over Rocky's head'

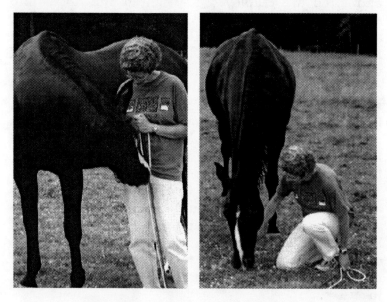

Friendly Game at Liberty

Application of Natural Horsemanship Principles in My Life

When I saw Susan working with Rocky in the 'friendly game' it spoke to me about the kind of close friendship God wants to have with me, where no matter what is happening around me, I don't get anxious, fearful or distracted, but focus on God's love and draw strength and courage from Him. 'Fear of the dark' was a big stumbling block to my mind and body being at peace. This was a fear that began as a child as early as I can remember, and continued to haunt me in my adult life. I experienced numerous nightmares and panic attacks, due to a vivid imagination, and most of all, a lack of trust. The dark represented evil lurking, ready to attack! When fear gripped me I certainly wanted to run. I actually did run away from home before I graduated from high school, but my stepfather made me return, but then I ran away again during the summer after my graduation. In my adult years when my husband was working night shifts I remember keeping a bat under my bed in case of an intruder at night. Fear had a way of sneaking into my life, creating more defenses and putting me into bondage.

God's desire for me was to set me free from fear so I could experience His love and peace. For this to happen I had to let Him into some of my more sensitive areas. I wanted to trust the God who knew all about my fears and where they came from. I began to spend much time in prayer and reading the scriptures. I found all the places in the Bible where fear was mentioned and came to realize I was listening to lies and letting them deeply affect my soul.

God revealed to me why I was so vulnerable to the dark, for example, because I was always watching scary television shows late at night when I was babysitting all by myself. I also allowed my imagination to run wild instead of shutting it off and focusing on something lovely and true. I had a critical attitude about life and saw things in a negative way that distorted the truth. I did suffer from watching physical abuse in the home as a child and sometimes suffered the affliction myself, thus causing most of my panic attacks and reoccurring nightmares, even after I left home for university and entered married life.

As a child I remember being trained to behave, much the same way that trainers normally train horses, by force and intimidation, which produces a fear and flight reflex. I was trying to fight the battle of fear on my own, rather than asking God to help me and deliver me from all of my fears and troubles. Trust was a major issue for me as it had been broken many times when I was a child. I began to learn that God's thoughts and ways were exactly opposite to mine and to the world's, for He sees all and knows all from a greater vantage point because He is our Creator.

Whenever I came to the end of myself, I willingly chose to trust God and to make myself vulnerable to Him. He demonstrated His faithfulness and grace to me when I listened and obeyed his promptings. There were many things that God showed me to help set me free. He made a way for me to eventually leave home and support myself while going to University, but unfortunately I took many of the fears with me.

One time, well into my thirties, at 1:00 in the morning, He challenged me to go across the street where our horses were boarded and take off their fly masks, which I had forgotten to do. Tom was at work and the children were sleeping. I did not have a flashlight and decided to face my fear of the dark with God's help. Together we went over to a huge rolling pasture of several acres with trees all around the outside, a creek running through, manure piles dotted here and there and wild animals lurking in the bush. It was cougar, coyote, wolf and bear country in Thornhill, Maple Ridge, and I had to find the five horses in the dark without the aid of any light. When I was really quiet I could hear horses munching dewy grass. One by one, I bumped into each horse, warning them with a whistle as I walked, hoping they wouldn't startle and run away. In the end, I had five fly masks and trembling legs, but I had begun to conquer my enemy, the fear of darkness.

Field of horses where I went in the dark to remove their fly masks

Many times God encouraged me to go out into the dark by myself and walk around our house just focusing on God's presence and the friendliness of the dark. Sometimes I would even challenge myself to go down into our basement in the pitch dark to get the laundry, or canning. I wanted to practice walking in truth, using the courage God had given me.

As I let go and faced each fear head-on with God's help and guidance, I learned that there was nothing evil about darkness and that it has its own special sounds, sights and soothing effects. Fear is no longer a snare to my soul. I can now sleep peacefully in darkness and not have nightmares or wild thoughts running through my mind. I decided to completely trust God that I had nothing to fear in the dark because I believed in His perfect love and He became my comfort. I understand that this doesn't mean something bad will never happen to me, because I have had my share of serious accidents. It was simply a great breakthrough for me to spiritually let go of my fear of the dark to experience God's grace and the truth. I would rather live in the freedom of the truth than in bondage to lies.

Biblical Application

II Timothy 1:7
"For God has not given us a spirit of fear, but of power and of love and of a sound mind."

I John 4:18
"There is no fear in love; but perfect love casts out fear, because fear involves torment. But he who fears has not been made perfect in love."

Psalm 23:4
King David wrote, *"Yea, though I walk through the valley of the shadow of death, I will fear no evil; for You are with me; Your rod and Your staff, they comfort me."*

Psalm 139:23-24
King David wrote, *"Search me, O God, and know my heart; try me, and know my anxieties; and see if there is any wicked way in me, and lead me in the way everlasting."*

17.

Other Games that Teach

*A*fter the 'join up' Susan did not want me to ride Rocky until we had done all the proper preparation on the ground, such as playing the six games of dominance: the porcupine game, driving game, circling game, yo-yo game, squeeze game and sideways game. We agreed that my family was much too important to me to have another accident where I could be seriously hurt or killed. Susan would demonstrate and lead each game for me, and then I would practice with Rocky, usually getting all tangled up in the rope. I was a bumbling greenhorn who was still threatened by Rocky's great strength, size and bad attitude. I needed to take leadership and establish boundaries with Rocky so he would learn not to come into my personal space without permission. He needed to let me lead him through various exercises that we would win together, so we could move on to a greater harmony of trust and respect.

In working with Rocky, Susan encouraged me to have the right attitude as a leader, demonstrating firmness, fairness, gentleness, patience and courage. She would always remind me when I showed the slightest sign of nervousness, fear or apprehension. This stretching process for Rocky and I was important for developing our emotional fitness and partnership. Rocky would be given small tasks to test his willingness to trust and yield to me in preparation for greater tasks and responsibilities and I would learn to be a leader in this partnership.

Preparing for playing the games

Clear communication and timing are the tools for all the games. The first game of dominance (one of two that I will discuss) is called the 'porcupine' game. For example, if I wanted to move Rocky backwards I would apply pressure to the front part of his face with my two fingers. To lower his head I would apply pressure right behind the ears, and to move Rocky's front end around I would apply pressure at his head and mid-section. This game taught Rocky to follow a feel and to let me into his personal space.

I would apply consistent pressure, politely asking him to move away from the pressure. The principle is one of 'set up' and 'wait' for a response, not quitting. When I worked in zone one around his head, being extremely defensive and sensitive, Rocky would react by putting his head up, ears back and would sometimes try to bite or escape! It was not about me versus Rocky, but about me gently gaining his respect and trust. As soon as he responded by moving away, he would receive comfort from me by using the friendly game of rubbing him and releasing the pressure quickly.

It's very important to know that there are four phases of 'friendly firmness' where the energy level goes up when asking the horse to yield. Susan refers to these phases as the pressure of a mosquito, then a fly, then a blackbird and finally, an eagle. Eventually, Rocky preferred the comfort and reward of pressure release and the friendliness of rubbing compared to the process of persistent asking, then telling and finally, promising. In every session we had with Rocky, he started by wanting to retain his dominance throughout all the games, but little by little he softened toward me.

Porcupine Game at Liberty

Porcupine Game on moving the front legs

Porcupine Game on the front end

Driving Game on the hind end

Yo-Yo Game

Application of Natural Horsemanship Principles in My Life

This picture of rebellion in Rocky reminded me of my own life as a child and into my adult years. I was often rebellious and challenging towards male authority, probably due to a strict upbringing where harshness and punishment caused fear and a lack of respect in me. That was a picture of my old nature, even though I belonged to God. I was not living as a child of God should, being a new person in Christ Jesus. God gradually began to change my heart by strong tugs from the Holy Spirit. It was time to start listening and responding to God, to follow a feel, that is, His leadership in my life.

In 1977, while I was in Amsterdam, Holland, preparing for the World Rowing Championships, I received a surprise phone call at the hotel where our Canadian team was staying. My sister, Marie, informed me that my birth father, with whom I had never had a relationship, due to his early departure from my mother's life before I was born, was soon to pass away from pneumonia and other complications.

My sister had felt a strong tug on her heart to go and read God's word and pray for him, but he was resistant to my sister's request. All his life he had suffered guilt, shame and rejection because of his wrong choices and relationships. I was told that he had spent many years in prison for his life of crime and that he had also spent time in a mental institution, one time receiving electric shock therapy. I knew so little of him because he only briefly came in and out of my life, trying to offer me little gifts of reconciliation whenever my stepfather was not present or my Nana arranged our meeting together. My sister wanted to introduce him to the forgiveness and unconditional love of the Lord Jesus. She wanted him to experience the same wonderful peace, love and joy that we had when the Holy Spirit sealed our eternal future in God at a young age.

My sister's news hit me very hard as I realized time was short to do anything about my relationship with my father. As I reflected over all my past memories of fear and confusion my first thought was to resist my sister's request. She implored each of us four siblings to forgive our father for all his past failures and hurts toward our family. I remember crying and realizing how much God had forgiven me and I knew God wanted me to forgive my father.

The next day, Marie went to our father and shared how each of his four children had totally forgiven him. His heart then opened up to God's love and forgiveness and he repented and prayed for forgiveness. He passed on a few days later. My sister received confirmation of our father's spiritual condition through a vivid dream some weeks later. She saw our father, Albert, walking into the arms of Jesus, because he was indeed in heaven with his Lord and Savior. I am so grateful to my sister for responding to God's tug on her heart to phone each of us and to minister to our father in his last days. That spiritual tug was like a 'porcupine' wake-up call to my heart to learn to forgive.

Many years later, another major change came into my heart because of a spiritual tug from the Lord. I grew up with a step-dad from the age of three in our family of four children, which later became seven children. In his late sixties, after retirement, he contracted emphysema and was in intensive care for the last three months of his life. Just before my stepfather died I remember God again gently applying pressure to my heart, softening me and reminding me of how much He had forgiven me and how great His unconditional love was towards me. He challenged me to forgive my stepfather for his treatment of me and to ask his forgiveness for my disobedience and rejection of him.

He was on his deathbed with a tube in his throat for breathing. It was in this desperate situation that I had my first opportunity to speak to him truthfully about our relationship without fear of reaction and with the hope of a softening in him so we could find peace in God's forgiveness together. He had tears in his eyes and nothing needed to be said.

Those gentle tugs, like the 'porcupine game' with Rocky, were the work of the Holy Spirit calling me to yield to His truth and His ways. The less I resisted God, the more I walked in freedom, experiencing peace, joy and love in my own heart. The power of forgiveness is truly amazing! Little did I realize that a root of bitterness toward both of my fathers had sprung up in me and caused me many problems with regard to having compassion for others and totally accepting them as God does. I am learning that His ways are perfect and all His ways are just.

Biblical Application

Colossians 3:12-15
"Therefore, as the elect of God, holy and beloved, put on tender mercies, kindness, humility, meekness, longsuffering; bearing with one another, and forgiving one another, if anyone has a complaint against another; even as Christ forgave you, so you also must do. But above all these things put on love, which is the bond of perfection. And let the peace of God rule in your hearts. . ."

18.

Focus and Discipline

*A*fter a time of teaching Rocky the seven games, we decided to move the round pen to a large open field of tall grass. It was time to test Rocky's respect toward me by letting him experience more freedom and a change of environment. Horses have great peripheral vision so they can detect the slightest movement as well as any smell or noise around them. On one side of the field a large thick forest of evergreens and deciduous trees loomed over us. In the past Rocky had seen many wild animals, such as cougar, bear and deer lurking in the bush and sometimes stalking out onto the pasture.

Susan wanted to prepare Rocky and I for riding in the saddle again. Her goal was to raise his trust and respect level and to gain his focus, so his old nature of fear and flight would not become an issue no matter what the surroundings were like. I had my concerns about this location. Everything was going so well at the original location that I hated to disturb the progress. Susan always reminded me that Rocky had a lot of inward emotional stress that needed to come out and be healed, so change and challenge were essential to strengthening his emotional fitness. I knew this was also true of my own life and so I was willing to trust Susan's judgment of Rocky's needs.

It was while doing an exercise called 'lateral lunging,' where Rocky was moving on the end of a twenty-foot line in a circular fashion at a walk, trot and canter, that I learned a huge lesson. I thought Rocky was doing well and showing much improvement in calmness and obedience during this time of greater freedom, but my reverie was interrupted when Susan called out to me, "Rocky is not respecting you! What are you going to do about it?"

Circling Game: Rocky is looking out disrespectfully

I was shocked when Susan pointed out to me that Rocky had his head turned out away from me in disrespect, not able to follow my lead. His focus was on the woods and elsewhere that a 'monster' might jump out at him. I asked Susan to demonstrate what I should do about it, because she had such an amazing way with Rocky. When she stepped into the ring and took her position in the center, holding the carrot stick and lunge line, he certainly paid attention. Rocky turned like a soldier to salute her with his massive body, ready to move at her slightest request. Like a flash he darted to the outside of the ring and focused on Susan's every movement. Susan was careful to reward Rocky with comfort by not staring at his head or driving him with her body language (energy).

At first Rocky was very tense, even when focused on her, as fear was his motivator. In time, Rocky relaxed and found comfort when he realized Susan was only communicating gentleness and calmness. When a noise or movement in the bush diverted Rocky's focus, Susan would try to draw his attention back to her by a quick 'bump' on the end of the rope, a fair but firm disciplinary measure. After a few bumps, Rocky still did not turn his focus to Susan, so she increased the discipline with a quick rise in energy while driving him to work on the outside of the circle. Just as Susan predicted, Rocky got tired of struggling and working on the outside of the ring and eventually he turned his head ever so slightly, looking for comfort. Susan immediately rewarded his acknowledgement of her as Alpha and then proceeded to ask Rocky to come in for comfort and rest.

One day, as I was lunging Rocky, he was startled by something unseen in the bushes. He pulled the rope out of my hands and bounded down the pasture with the long rope bouncing behind him like a monster in pursuit. Our two dogs, Bud and Julie, bounded after Rocky at his heals, barking and causing greater confusion. Rocky came to a trembling halt with the rope pulled against his legs. His fear and independence certainly got him into trouble. I was glad to have been on the ground and not on his back. His old nature had returned when his focus got off of me and onto his fears. *Will Rocky and I ever reach our destination?* I wondered.

Horses' temperaments are often described by the way their eyes look. Eyes are said to be the window to the soul and can communicate all our emotions. As with humans so it is with horses. The more time I spent in gaining Rocky's focus the more I noticed a change in his eyes from challenging to soft and trusting. Focus for horses involves their mind, will and emotions and it begins with their eyes and body posture. I was desirous of Rocky's undivided attention so I could lead in our relationship and gain his true loyalty.

Application of Natural Horsemanship Principles to My Life

Here I was, trying to train Rocky to focus on me when I had trouble focusing on God.

Throughout a major portion of my life, I focused solely on competitive running and later on rowing. God was patient with me and definitely used my focus on running in my teen years to keep me out of trouble, provide me with good friends and build strong character in me. As my narrow focus in competitive sports continued into later years I suffered many repercussions. One of the negative aspects of years of high-pressure training and constant competition was the surge of adrenalin that kicked in whenever I started to get anxious about racing or performing. Over time, this adrenalin surge continued even when I had ceased my competitive rowing career. My mind had trained my body to react in the fear and flight mode towards any pressure or performance. I eventually developed health problems from the constant adrenalin surges. Being a success was important to my ego, because I did not want to experience failure or loss of identity.

I was always a daydreamer who loved to wander off in thought to a better life and create my own world. People would talk to me and my mind would be somewhere else, not even listening to their conversation. My focus was on myself, that is, my needs and my desires. Performance in sports became my claim to fame, my road to success and my sole focus and ambition. Yes, I gained much in friendships, character development and life experiences through training, competition and traveling. However, I also lost much in developing relationships with the people who meant the most in my life, such as my family and the Lord Jesus.

In various ways God's love brought discipline to change my self-centered life. He allowed me to experience much physical discomfort from stress in my body. He allowed me to bear a heavy load of loneliness and struggle in trying to stay on top of running and rowing. I was building a false sense of identity, security and value, so I had no true peace, joy, or satisfaction in life. Life was uncomfortable for me when I was focused on building my own kingdom and trying to provide for myself.

Eventually, through much good mentoring and teaching in the Word of God, I discovered that my true identity and comfort were not based on my performance and accomplishments, but on God's value for me as one of His children, "fearfully and wonderfully made." I realized that I was fully accepted and loved by my Heavenly Father. What God thought of me was more important than what any person thought of me. God would continue to "grow me up" and change my heart as I focused more on Him. He would provide all I needed and more as I trusted in Him. God did not call me to be successful, but to be faithful.

My husband and I decided that in raising our children we would never pressure them into a high level of competitive sports, but rather encourage them to diversify their interests and become more broadminded. We hoped and prayed that their focus would be knowing God, pursuing godly leadership, caring about people and serving God's greater plans and purposes for them. Only God knew what that would look like, and so we would allow them much freedom to explore many avenues in life, not pressuring them to go down the narrow road of elitism.

Howard Family and Sports
from the Sun Newspaper (1987)

None of our very athletically inclined and gifted children have regretted not going into full time sports. Francine proved to be a very good field hockey player and runner. Courtney was a top runner in college in Alberta and Andrew became a top runner in the BC Track Championships. They all love running and sports, but their hearts are focused on the Lord's will for their lives. Francine, our eldest, and her husband and two sons now serve God in southwest China. Courtney, our second daughter, is studying at Trinity Western University with the hopes of continuing in overseas missionary work. Andrew is 19, and is open to God's leading in his life, preferably in the industry of fishing, wildlife and forestry. He knows how to work hard and creatively earn money even when the economy is poor. Grace, our surprise child when I turned forty, is eleven, and very missions minded with a heart to possibly join her sister one day in China. Presently she supports missionaries who work with orphan children in Haiti.

My family at White Rock beach (Fall 2004)

*Tom and grandson, Clay; Grace and our grandson Ty;
and their mom, Francine, and myself with Annie*

My focus is to know God, to be strong in Him
and to serve Him with my whole heart and desire.
God doesn't require my performance of what I can do
for Him, but rather, He only desires my willingness
to trust and obey Him. This may sound foolish to the
world's ways, but my fear of failure and rejection are
gone because of His unconditional love and
acceptance. Focus and discipline are important in
my relationship with God. His loving discipline keeps
me true to Him.

Biblical Application

Hebrews 12:5b-6

*"My son, do not despise the chastening of the
Lord, nor be discouraged when you are rebuked by*

Him; for whom the Lord loves He chastens, and scourges every son whom He receives."

Psalm 32:8

"I will instruct you and teach you in the way you should go; I will guide you with My eye."

Psalm 16:8

"I have set the Lord always before me; because He is at my right hand I shall not be moved."

Isaiah 45:22

"Look to Me, and be saved, all you ends of the earth! For I am God, and there is no other."

19

Higher Levels of Trust

*T*he day finally came when I needed to get on Rocky's back and begin applying everything that I had learned on the ground with him. The first time I mounted him was without a saddle, since we still had much more work to do to prepare Rocky for the saddle. Susan introduced me to a very foreign way of riding Rocky. Not only was he to trust me, but I also needed to trust him even more while I sat bareback without the aid of stirrups, a horn and a bridle. I was to learn how to be sensitive to Rocky by using a light string halter and a 12-foot rope on one side of him.

This seemed like a very strange set-up and I distinctly remember feeling extremely vulnerable to Rocky because I did not have the usual controls. Again I had to face my greatest fear of being 'out of control' and possibly falling off. Susan told me not to even go there with my thoughts. I was to focus on what we were trying to accomplish and not let fear dominate my mind. My attitude was to be positive in trusting Rocky because he had learned everything well on the ground and we were ready to move on to this next phase. Rocky was changing. My emotional fitness was still not mended by any means, so I greatly depended upon Susan's support and guidance, and of course God's greater purposes for me.

Starting out bareback with one rope, no bridle

My first instinct when I got on Rocky was to pull the rope firm to feel for control when he tensed up and raised his head in apprehension. Susan quickly reminded me to loosen the rope and give him freedom to communicate trust and relaxation. I was fighting an immense battle in my emotions and mind to not take control. I decided to follow the plan and see what would happen. As I sat quietly and made a concerted effort to relax and trust Rocky, he gradually relaxed and brought his head down to a comfortable position. We both breathed a big sigh of relief.

Before walking forward, Susan showed me how to put Rocky in the 'neutral lateral position' by asking for his head to bend to the side. I gently lifted the single rope up high and slowly ran my other hand down the rope. I then drew the rope out and around to my knee, asking for his head to follow the feel of the rope and yield to my request. This request was a big test of Rocky's trust in me because I was asking him to completely make himself vulnerable to predator attack. I was asking for him to turn his head and neck all the way around as far as my foot. In doing this, Rocky couldn't see anything but me. This action is not natural for a prey animal. Rocky resisted. I found myself wanting to pull his head around instead of asking politely for a yield. It was like a tug-o-war of strength, a battle of wills—me against Rocky where he would gradually build up resistance and win.

Neutral Lateral Position: showing trust while vulnerable

In time, as I learned to ask politely and release quickly to reward his try, Rocky began to respond well. I felt bad for Rocky who had to put up with my awkwardness of learning something new while teaching him. Rocky was very forgiving as he soon learned to simply 'follow a feel' that was extremely light. He became more sensitive to my movements and I was delightfully rewarded for taking the risk of trusting him.

Trust and Respect

Susan very strongly warned me that this part of 'natural horsemanship' was the most important lesson for us to learn in case of an emergency because at such a time I would need to keep him quiet and confident in me. If I were ever to ride on the roads and trails again I would have to learn how to stop my horse and refocus his attention on me. And before we would leave to go on a ride I would have to test Rocky's attitude with this 'neutral lateral position' to see if he was willing to quietly listen and obey. In other words, was he soft or resistant to my requests? This higher level of trust, riding bareback without a bridle, would lead to greater harmony in our long-term relationship.

Trust and Vulnerability 3 years later

Application of Natural Horsemanship Principles in My Life

There have been many times in my life when God has asked me to be vulnerable in order to follow Him. Like Rocky, my old nature was to stay in control so I would not be vulnerable to others or risk failure. But God has won my confidence and I am gradually learning to trust Him in the more difficult areas of faith where I need to be completely vulnerable and let go of my fears.

I recall a very scary incident when the Holy Spirit encouraged me to share my faith in God with a complete stranger. I distinctly remember going up to a Hell's Angels biker in White Rock where my friend, Donna, and I had pulled into a gas station. God gave me a burden for this guy's bleak future and his ignorance in what he was doing to himself and others for the sake of his identity in this biker club. In fear and trembling, I simply walked up to him and very boldly told him as kindly as possible that the Bible says that hell and Satan are real. I also told him that the Bible says heaven and God are real too and that God loved him and he needed to look to God for help. He didn't say a word; he was so stunned at my bold approach.

In a few seconds I was gone in my car wondering how I dared to warn and challenge this man. Deep down I had peace, knowing that I had responded to the gentle 'tug of the Holy Spirit,' asking me to be vulnerable and to trust his request. I sensed a real partnership with God in that venture. God knows everything, including a man's heart and his destiny. I had to trust that I played a vital role in obeying and trusting God's quiet voice within me.

One of the most vulnerable times in my life was in 2001 when I sensed God's call to do something unusual—to go to South Korea to seek out a ministry opportunity to serve God. Before I explain what happened in South Korea, however, let me give a little background on my experience and training in Christian ministry that had prepared me step-by-step for this unusual call.

After retirement from rowing I stayed home to raise our four children, which allowed me to attend many seminars on marriage, raising a family and maturing in God. I completed almost two years of Bible School at White Rock Christian Fellowship, under Pastors Verne and Marge Wilson and John and Lyza Clarke. For thirteen years at this very stable loving church I was able to get rooted in God's love and sound Bible doctrine. This excellent discipleship training gave me confidence to lead many ministries over the past twenty-five years, such as ladies' Bible studies, children's Bible clubs, Sunday School, youth group ministries, prayer groups and teaching on the creation/evolution controversy.

None of my past ministry experience and training had any cross-cultural involvement until we moved to Maple Ridge in 1989. A Christian woman, who later became a very good friend, approached me to work as a coordinator with Cultural Homestay International for teaching Japanese students. I was thrilled to have this opportunity to work with Japanese students. Two programs later, a friend and myself decided to create our own ESL organization working with Christian host families. Shortly after this ESL project got underway our family moved to Vancouver Island and I ended up home schooling Korean students for ESL as a Christian ministry through contacts with my Korean sister-in-law. Our daughter Grace was born a year later, however, and my work with foreign students in our home was postponed indefinitely.

Despite all my work with Japanese students, I had never been to Asia, nor had I considered going there. So my response to God's call to go to South Korea became quite an adventure of faith. It was like stepping out of the boat to 'walk on water,' something I had most definitely not done before! Taking this risk had the potential of making me look very foolish, but then again, it was only through taking risks that I had ever made any substantial gains in life.

The call to go was confirmed in many different ways. I would only go if my close teaching friend, Penny Galliazzo, would agree to accompany me, which she did. Also, my family was willing to let me go, which meant covering for me for a week and a half of absence from doing all the farm chores, housework, meals, driving, looking after the children, and so on. Thirdly, our church was very interested in establishing an international ministry with Christian leaders overseas, so they were willing to prayerfully support our venture.

Lastly, there was a Korean professor, Dr. Paul Yang, at Trinity Western University whom I had never met, but vaguely remembered having his contact number. We felt to arrange a meeting with him, to seek his advice on our venture of faith, and when we did, he encouraged us to go to Korea because the need was great. Little did we realize that this Professor was going to be the key person to introduce us to the people who would be most interested in our ministry.

A week before leaving for Korea our pick up and drop off at the airport was finally arranged through a contact in Vancouver. We had no itinerary, only strangers to meet and two places to stay. My Korean sister-in-law asked her family and friends to help orientate us in Korea and to host us when possible. Even though we were not in control of our daily schedule, we had peace. The funds came through and so our flights were booked! No turning back now! Right up until the last day we did not have all our accommodation confirmed. It was important that we stay with people and not in hotels, if possible, because we needed a personal guide.

When we arrived in Korea we were asked what our itinerary was for two weeks and we simply said, " We don't know, but we're trusting in God." Our driver then regrettably informed us that our accommodation was changed and we would have to stay at Ewha Women's University on the outskirts of Seoul. Penny and I were surprised at the sudden change and knew that we would really have to depend on God now. Somehow we still managed to connect with all the people Professor Paul Yang had contacted for us, but also with many more. The Korean people we met were wonderful hosts who really took care of our needs and blessed us abundantly. We were fascinated by the Korean culture, which was so radically different from ours. Our hearts were burdened when we saw how much the youth and their parents suffered under the demands and pressures of a highly competitive society where success and performance are very important to one's individual worth and happiness.

Penny and I in Korea on our first trip

A few months later, during the summer, our first interested Korean visitors arrived to check out our credentials, doctrine of faith, the Comox Valley, our facilities, our program, and our vision. That winter our Church established a ministry called, GLEEM, Grace Life English Experience Ministry. We hosted twenty-nine Korean youth from a Christian ministry located just outside of Seoul. Two years later, GLEEM became a society and was renamed "God's Loving English Experience Ministry."

Since GLEEM's inception, I was given the honor of Directorship, and with it, all the responsibilities and rewards of working with staff, host families and Korean Christian leaders and Pastors. In three years, GLEEM has hosted nine programs for Korean youth during the fall, winter, spring and summer seasons. The students have returned to Korea greatly enriched by the abundance and beauty of the Comox Valley, the nurture and love from their host families and the discipleship and training in GLEEM to further their relationship with God and with one another. GLEEM staff and host families have also greatly benefited from having the Korean students and their leaders influence our lives.

Korean students (Fall 2003)

Beginning a new work always has its struggles and blessings. Many times GLEEM has almost fallen apart due to cross-cultural crisis in communication and relationships, but God has taken hold of the vision and revived it for His great purposes. I have learned so much about walking in faith, trusting God and listening to His voice through this ministry. I have always admired our forefathers who pioneered a living out of the Canadian wilderness with little experience. Out of their dedication, hard work and spirit of adventure a nation was born to be a blessing to other nations. GLEEM is similarly fashioned for the purpose of beginning a new work, that of letting Korean youth experience something new and liberating apart from schoolwork and exams.

After spending five months in Canada, the Korean youth have their minds expanded, their hearts deeply touched and their future goals challenged. They have learned that developing relationship with God and with one another is far more important than their performance and success in life. The pressure comes off and they are ready to go back home to pioneer their own new beginnings. Penny and I and others from GLEEM have returned to Korea to follow up on the students' lives. We have witnessed wonderful fruit as we see Christian maturity, joy, peace and strong relationships formed with their fellow students, causing a further ripple effect to their peers and family.

I am so glad that I heard God's quiet voice urging me to trust Him to go to Korea to discover His heart. In the natural, this idea seemed completely absurd because we followed very few of the normal procedures for beginning a new business. Much to the amazement of many onlookers, we headed off to Korea having done no advertising or promotional work. I have definitely discovered that being vulnerable and taking risks are all part of experiencing His grace. Everything in my life has brought me to this point of glorifying God through walking in faith. How blessed I am to be living on the cutting edge of a breakthrough into something great!

Biblical Application

II Corinthians 9:8
"And God is able to make all grace abound toward you, that you, always having all sufficiency in all things, may have an abundance for every good work."

II Corinthians 5:7
"For we walk by faith, not by sight."

20.

Working at Liberty

*S*ome of my most fun times with Rocky are not when I am riding him, but when we play together (groundwork). This form of play is done at 'liberty' when Rocky is completely free in the large riding ring. I send Rocky out to run about at his own free will. He usually gets quite excited and tears up the ground pretty good with his kicks, bucks, sliding stops and sudden turns. It is fun to see him full of life and 'liberty.' I do not need the carrot stick, a lead rope, or a halter to control him. Rocky is free to respond to me with his heart and desire as he wishes.

Working at liberty is a real test of his relationship with me. I have even successfully played this 'liberty' game with Rocky out in the large open field. Out there I usually wait until he is not so rambunctious or distracted before beckoning him in to me with a wave of my hand. He picks up the signal quickly and responds by turning in and slowly walking towards me, usually a little at a time. He faces me squarely, pausing for the next signal as a sign of respect. When he runs beside me around the ring and jumps with me over cavaleties (jumps), we are truly partners. At my request, he will circle around me, side pass away from me and back up, all at liberty, with no restraints, only body communication. Sometimes, Rocky takes off in a great burst of speed and then playfully comes back for more. He knows that he is free to leave or come.

At Liberty Rocky comes to the mounting block

At Liberty we are partners
Rocky comes to the mounting block for me

One day, on two different occasions, while at liberty, Rocky demonstrated great boldness and enthusiasm in responding to my request to do something very different and more challenging. My friend, Betty, watched the entire scene. Rocky and I were at opposite ends of the ring. I beckoned for him to come to me by going over two cavaleties while enroute. He looked at me solidly for a long moment as I was coaxing him. His head lowered and his eyes softened as he responded to my invitation. Rocky had never gone over obstacles without me running beside him. He could have easily gone around the obstacles, or avoided me; instead, he walked straight over the low jumps towards me. I was overjoyed at his willing response. Rocky wanted to please me.

A second time, when Susan was watching Rocky and I play at liberty, Rocky totally surprised us both with his boldness. I wasn't sure of Rocky's intentions the first time, until he did it again to prove to me his respect. Rocky was running in a very playful manner, kicking up his heels and frolicking around with glee like a child. It was quite a sight to behold! When I was separated a good distance across the ring from him, I motioned Rocky to come. He turned to face me first and then as if he had a second thought, he pranced and bounded with great energy towards me until he came to a sliding halt with his two front legs firmly planted in a salute fashion. We stood eyeball to eyeball. My eyes popped out in surprise and we both laughed at Rocky's antics. I wasn't afraid when Rocky bounded toward me, seemingly out of control, because I saw his self-control and friendliness.

It was like he was saying, "Look how close I can come into your space without hurting you." He seemed to entreat me as he finished by lowering his head. I rubbed his forehead in comfort and acceptance. Those were very special moments of great trust and respect with Rocky at liberty.

Application of Natural Horsemanship Principles in My Life

This picture of Rocky playing while at liberty, displaying confident and bold behavior toward me, reminds me of how God wants me to be in relationship with Him. As a child I viewed God as distant and impersonal. When I did something wrong I saw Him as the Judge, quick to condemn and punish when I did wrong. I feared God, not with a healthy respect, or awe, but with worry about how He saw me. When I made a mess of things, or failed in some endeavor, I didn't think of running to God for help or comfort because I did not feel safe with Him at those times.

Thankfully, later in my adult Christian life I discovered the real God, the God of the Bible, who loves unconditionally, no matter how much I fail to measure up to his standards. I came to realize that I am free to be me and to fail, since God will not make me bend to His ways because He accepts me just as I am and is constantly inviting me to be in relationship with Him. He knows my weaknesses and all about me, so there is nothing to hide from Him. The more I know Him, the more I want to open my heart to Him, to let Him come close, even allowing Him to discipline me, knowing His will for me is better than my own.

Now that I feel safe with God, I can run boldly and confidently into His presence, like a child. No matter what my state, God has become my encourager. This is the father that I have always wanted and needed in my life. I had never been able to have an intimate relationship based on trust and respect until I truly understood God's relationship with me. It is hard to imagine that God, my Father, the Creator and Ruler of the Universe, is truly interested in me! All He really wants from me is my 'heart and desire,' so I can glorify Him in my life as my Creator, Lord and Savior.

Biblical Application

Psalm 86:15
"But You, O Lord, are a God full of compassion, and gracious, longsuffering and abundant in mercy and truth."

Ephesians 3:12
"...in whom we have boldness and access with confidence through faith in Him."

Hebrews 4:16
"Let us therefore come boldly to the throne of grace, that we may obtain mercy and find grace to help in time of need."

21.

Saddling Up!

*F*acing my greatest fear with Rocky was something I really wanted to avoid, but I knew it was inevitable. I hated the prospect of failure and disappointment with saddling Rocky. It had been nine months of solid consistent training the 'natural way' with Susan, and Leslie as her helper. Two weeks before my first big trip to Korea, Susan decided that it was the right time to saddle up Rocky and face the inevitable.

We were so encouraged by Rocky's change in demeanor. He had become very relaxed and gentle in response to the new training so we decided to go for it and saddle him up. As we began the saddling process Rocky surprisingly took the saddle well, with only slight hesitations. I even got out on the trails for four days of blissful riding in the saddle. However, every time I saddled him by myself I noticed his increased sensitivity and agitation, even though I was very methodical and careful not to be sneaky.

For example, the first time I put the saddle on Rocky, he fidgeted so much that the saddle slipped to the side causing him to step on the girth strap. I wrestled to hold the saddle back into place while trying to keep Rocky calm. The second time, he leaped forward almost as if the saddle surprised him. The third time, Rocky tensed up with his whole body going rigid and he jumped sideways. Susan instructed me to trot him out on the long line. Rocky was pumped with adrenalin and fear! Like a bullet train, he took off bucking and crow hopping all over the ring. He was scaring himself more and more, so I left the ring for safety. When a horse explodes everyone had better look out!

Walking Rocky before mounting in the saddle

Susan and I sat stunned as we watched Rocky lose all control of his emotions. It was always amazing that he never got caught in the ring line or jumped out. When exhausted, he stopped his frenzied bucking, and Susan went into the ring to direct him forward, but he began bucking all over again. We couldn't understand why he would react this way to a seemingly unprovoked situation. We were disappointed and frustrated at the outcome of nine months of training. It was concluded and agreed upon that I was not to ride Rocky with the saddle for now and maybe never. My first and very despairing reaction was, "I'll have to sell him to a really experienced cowboy, or worse, put him down."

Several weeks later, after I had spent soul-searching hours evaluating the situation, I started riding Rocky again, but bareback! I decided not to give up on Rocky, but to press on with him, regardless of his handicap and unexplained fear of the saddle. We continued on the journey of building Rocky's and my emotional fitness and strengthened our relationship. There was so much more to learn together and enjoy, regardless of the saddling problem. Whether Rocky's reaction to the saddle was a physical or emotional problem, we would never know, unless it was somehow made very evident to us. I made the final decision that I was committed to Rocky and to Susan's training, because I could definitely see that it was proving to be good for both of us.

Someone once said that in handling problems, 80% is your attitude, while 20% is actually the problem. We could have tried more forceful measures with Rocky, but deep down I knew that my relationship with Rocky, which was built on trust and respect, was something I did not want to forfeit. I did not want to discipline him for something he might not have been able to overcome. Rocky had learned to yield in every area of training except for the saddling, so I gave him the benefit of the doubt that he had a true physical problem that handicapped his ability to be saddled.

Just over a year later, Susan and I decided to try a new and better-fitting saddle on Rocky, an Australian endurance saddle, thinking how gentle it would be on his withers and huge shoulder muscles. The fit was perfect, so it would be a good test of whether the problem was the girth or the saddle pressure. We went through all the proper preparations of playing the seven games and desensitizing him with the saddle. Rocky seemed to accept everything in a relaxed manner and I was encouraged. We left the saddle on him for 2 hours one day in the riding ring to give him lots of time to see how harmless the saddle was. We were pleased that he did not buck.

The next day, while on my own, I went through all the same saddling routine with him. After I finished doing up the girth strap Rocky tensed as he stepped forward with me. He instantly went straight up in the air, almost over backwards. He was like a massive object looming directly over my head ready for a strike. When he came down, he bolted forward, crow hopping. Our two dogs, Julie and Bud, joined in from nearby and a big bucking and kicking session continued to the other side of the ring, where Rocky eventually stopped, head down, with the lead rope on the ground. The dogs reluctantly came back to me. I slowly walked towards Rocky, determined not to quit, and did the saddle up tighter so it would not slip sideways. After picking up the rope, I asked him to trot forward, but the bucking continued. I abruptly turned away and left him to think about it for two hours. What a disappointment! My husband was leaning over the fence witnessing the last bucking routine. He saw my exasperation and felt the same.

I have prayed and thought a great deal about this dilemma with Rocky. What has God been trying to teach me? How could all this be of benefit when the outcome has been so disappointing? I am sure that most people can relate when they think about seemingly unsolvable problems in their lives. Susan's advice has been to be creative and to think of these obstacles not as winning or losing matches, but as opportunities to grow and learn by. This strikes a chord in my heart, because we cannot control everything that happens. Many situations are bigger than us and not always within our grasp to understand or fix.

I have come to understand that God is far greater than my problem and I have peace over the situation, because I know that God is more interested in my attitude and response than in my winning over Rocky. I am still open today about solving this problem, but until God gives me a fresh insight I am going to focus on building our relationship in other areas, since Rocky has so many wonderful attributes to enjoy. I see Rocky as a special gift from God to help train me to learn more about Him.

Application of Natural Horsemanship Principles in my Life

This frustrating scenario with Rocky reminds me of my own ongoing fears that I would love to have victory over—things that often embarrass me or cause me great problems at times. People are surprised when I share about my fears. They think of me as strong and capable of whatever I set my mind to because of my Olympic background in rowing and all round sports ability. But I am truly paranoid when it comes to the thought of falling, speed, heights and getting lost! Many times, since working with Rocky, I have been challenged to face the fear of falling. I have had many falls off horses and been seriously injured and even nearly killed! I have fallen and crashed badly in skiing, during sledding, running, hurdling, and in gymnastics in elementary school. The very thing I fear seems to keep happening to me. I am so thankful that God is in control of my life and He never gives up on me, despite my weaknesses and failures.

In the past few years I have learned to focus more on God and less on my fears. Tom and I, with my cousin and her husband, Susan and Jim, have gone on yearly wilderness treks for several days at a time where I have had to overcome fears like crossing a river on a high narrow log or on a swinging bridge. Other times it has been scaling a cliff with a rope to climb up because of a high tide, or climbing a narrow ridge or high peak. By facing my fears they have become less daunting, but they are something I may always have to battle.

My last terrible fall was in the year 2004, while leading a group of Korean youth on a snowshoe adventure on Mt. Washington. After having a bonfire with wieners and marshmallows for lunch we snowshoed further up the mountain, aiming for the radio tower. For fun, I sat on a round saucer, sliding down the logging road to meet up with the Korean students who were snowshoeing uphill. I was trapped on the spinning saucer as it kept getting closer to the edge, and then suddenly dropped out of sight over the cliff and proceeded towards an array of granite rocks and cedar trees. The flying saucer managed to swing around a huge granite rock because of a lip of snow, only to quickly smack me into a huge cedar tree and plunge me down a tree hole.

My body was so impacted that I could not move or speak for what seemed like a long period of time, even though my friend was calling to me from the top. Many thoughts raced through my mind, but the most important thought was that I did not die, nor did I sustain a head injury! My body felt extremely lifeless as I tried to just wiggle even an inch. What a predicament! How was I to get out of this hole?

My cousin, Susan, and two agile Korean boys came carefully down the steep and slippery slope to pry me from the tree hole. It was no use. My helpers were standing in four to five feet of soft, wet snow that would not enable them to move me; I would have to free myself. It was a grimacing moment, but I managed to wedge my good foot against the tree and push with all my might to elevate my body to where they could tie a rope on me. The two students pushed my good foot up the slope one small movement at a time, while the frightened and inexperienced Korean students on the top of the hill made a line to pull me up. If my bad leg, ribs or hip were even remotely moved I screamed in pain. However, knowing that pain was inevitable, I just continued with the process of shimmying up the snow bank until I reached the top, where I painfully lay down in the freezing snow while hypothermia rapidly took hold of my senses.

While the circle of students were crying and praying for me, I remembered my cell phone in my backpack. Someone dialed my husband's cell and then handed me the phone. It was an awkward moment as I tried to restrain my emotions and tell Tom that I was injured and needed rescuing off the mountain. My rescuer was on his way, but not soon enough as the cold increased. Thankfully, the students' prayers helped the pain to subside. Once again, God intervened at a critical moment in my life.

Several hours later, after a search and rescue crew, ambulance crew and my family had arrived, I was rescued by a police helicopter and taken to the nearby hospital. That episode hit the newspapers and the radio. Miraculously, God spared my life and kept me from having a broken hip and ribs, but the massive contusion on my hip and bruised ribs definitely slowed me down for a while!

Helicopter rescue on Mt. Washington (2004)

Another wild adventure in facing my fear of heights and falling took place on Whistler Mountain. I was enjoying a retreat with my past Olympic female rowing teammates when they challenged me to do the Zip Trek, a fairly new event at Whistler. It was the scariest challenge in heights for me. I literally remember shaking while standing glued to the ramp, not being able to jump off the 200-foot high platform to zip across 1200 meters over the Fitzimmons River. As I focused on God, I realized that this moment was the ultimate test in trusting Him for the ability to let go and jump. (I am sure it would be very similar to sky diving.) Most of my rowing friends did it with glee and with confidence, and some of them even hung upside down. I was very thrilled to complete the Zip Trek right side up. My emotional fitness had proven strong, thanks to God for bringing Susan and Natural Horsemanship into my life with Rocky.

My trainer, Susan, has been one of my greatest assets in working through my many fears with Rocky. In all of our sessions, which were weekly at times, Susan stretched my emotional fitness with her wise and discerning ways. In the natural, Susan has

great horse savvy (sense), as she is able
Rocky's behavior and win the games of
with him through gentleness and pat
appreciate her friendship, support a...
standards, wanting the best for both Rocky and I.
Safety is always a priority with Susan and so far I
have never been hurt during a lesson with Rocky.
Even if I were ever to fall off, which I nearly have
several times when Rocky decided to do a big buck
during a canter session in the ring, I know that
Susan would just smile, give a chuckle and
encourage me to get back on and refocus on the task
at hand.

In my life the Holy Spirit is the person, or agent,
that God uses to motivate, teach and correct me in
love, training me like a soldier for battle. My life, as it
is for everyone, is a spiritual battle with many
difficulties, challenges and dark times to wrestle in
my mind, will and emotions. My soul desires peace,
but not the peace the world gives, only the peace that
God gives which enables me to rise up to life's
challenges.

I feel very strongly that Susan was sent by God
to help me understand His spiritual principles of
truth and grace, which are so simply and clearly
demonstrated in Natural Horsemanship. Every
difficult thing, even my fall from Rocky, has worked
out for good, and ultimately for God's glory and
honor! I do not regret having started on this difficult
journey, because from the very beginning it was God
who gave me the peace to forge ahead into the
unknown territory of conquering every fear. I knew
that if God wanted me to work with Rocky, even
though there was a risk of getting hurt, then He
would give me the 'heart and desire' to follow and
trust His leading and direction, even when my fears
loomed bigger than my ability to face them.

Biblical Application

Romans 8:28

"And we know that all things work together for good to those who love God, to those who are the called according to His purpose."

James 1:2-4

"My brethren, count it all joy when you fall into various trials, knowing that the testing of your faith produces patience. But let patience have its perfect work, that you may be perfect and complete [meaning 'mature'], *lacking nothing."*

22.

Heart and Desire

*M*uch of my life was spent being relentlessly pursued by God. His irresistible love and passion captured my *heart and desire*. All my ambitions, hopes and dreams gradually became His. I eventually realized that I was born to be a delight to God and to others! As I yielded to His love, my cup of life was no longer seen as half empty, but overflowing with His joy, peace and love!

I have always wanted to live life to the fullest, and in my attempts to do so I have pursued many sports and challenges. It is interesting that God took the very simple *desires* that He put within me to show me my heart and to help shape my future.

From the time I was very young I remember expressing over and over again to my best friend that I had a strong desire to have a horse ranch when I grew up. Tom and I have never had a full-fledged ranch, but we have had over twenty-four horses in the past twenty-five years and at one point our family ran children's horse camps on our forty acres in Courtenay. We also gave horsemanship classes for beginners and small group trail rides. Many people have come to our place in the Comox Valley and enjoyed our horses in the private rural setting. I especially remember a very fun time when a group of home-schooled children came to learn about horses and our three horses became the guinea pigs while ten or so children brushed, petted, rode and gleaned all they could from those special lessons.

Sharing our horses was a tremendous vehicle for making friends in the community and developing my leadership skills. God also used my love and desire for horses to build in me His principles of relationship with Him and others. He was preparing me for a greater work.

Another desire I had at a very young age was to be a teacher. I used to come home from elementary school and play school with my friends and even by myself with imaginary pupils. In elementary school I often helped the teacher mark and grade papers. After six years of university I taught for only a short time and then we started our family. My professional teaching career disappeared for twenty years while I stayed home to raise our children. I was not disappointed at the loss of my career, however, because God gave me something better than teaching public school. He gave me the opportunity to home school our four children in Christian education during the various stages of their educational life, which in turn enhanced my foundations in the word of God. We had fun learning and growing together in love and faith. Throughout those home schooling years I experienced a deep desire to teach and minister to children and young adults, which later led me into pioneering a discipleship and training ministry for international students.

During the years I volunteered at a private Christian School I discovered that I had a deep, hidden desire to be a principal. At one time the opportunity came close, but we moved and so I pursued other interests as we helped plant a church in Maple Ridge. Two years later, when we moved to the Comox Valley in 1991, I was asked to home school other children, namely boys. I said, "Yes," since I wanted my son, Andrew to have school friends during those five years from grades five to nine. My husband renovated a garage on our forty-acre ranch for the little home school called Emmanuel, where I had a total of nine students in five different grades over a five-year period.

Immanuel Homeschool days on the farm
Adrian, Daniel, Andrew, Grace, Josh, Julie & Bud

The boys came early for farm chores and we started school at 10:00 am, finishing at 3:00 pm. There was a wood stove to keep us cozy, and the boys took turns splitting wood and kindling. They had many outside breaks where they explored the woods, built forts and played sports in the nearby pasture. On special sunny afternoons we would hop on our mountain bikes and head off to our favorite trail, doing a large loop home through various bumpy terrains. Again, without me knowing it, God had actually fulfilled my desire to become a principal, even if it was only for a one-room schoolhouse. I loved teaching and shepherding the boys during those precious times. It certainly built stamina and resiliency for future challenges in ministry.

It seems that God in His wisdom put desires into my heart as a child that would eventually play a major role in displaying God's purposes in and through me. As I complete the writing of this book, I am now fifty-two years of age and serving as the Director of GLEEM. It is a leadership position I never aspired to, nor sought out, but one that the Lord has definitely led me into. As I look back over my life I can see that He was preparing me for this position over a twenty-year period. In GLEEM, I am able to continue teaching all the subjects that I immensely enjoy, especially Creationism. Most of all, God has transformed my heart through the relationships I have had to develop and work with in the ministry.

As a leader I have experienced being on the front line of attack where I have been challenged to depend upon God for His strength, wisdom and courage. All of the Natural Horsemanship principles that I have discovered while working with Susan and Rocky have prepared me for this very overwhelming responsibility and privilege of working with host families, GLEEM staff, foreign teenage students and overseas Christian leaders. It is a daunting task that has required much hard work, discipline and perseverance, to which my running and rowing careers have greatly contributed. God knew and orchestrated every step of my life to lead me to this very time, my most fruitful season of serving God in the latter years of my life.

*With Dan, Sheila and Korean students
in Seosan, Korea (Fall 2004)*

*With Sheila and Korean students on our visit to Korea
(Fall 2004)*

The greatest reward for all the labor, pain and tears of serving in this vulnerable position of leadership is that it has caused me to see the true nature of God. He is a good God who knows all of my frailties and needs. He is my true source of peace, joy and strength. He is my comfort, and without His faithfulness and love I would never have achieved anything of worth. When people ask me, "How do you do it, Cheryl?" I want always to say, "It is only by the grace of God." Although I have been wonderfully gifted with good health, boundless energy, enthusiasm and creative ability, it was not until He captured my heart and desire that I began to live for a purpose far greater than myself!

Psalm 37:3-5; 7

"Trust in the Lord, and do good;
Dwell in the land, and feed on
His faithfulness.
Delight yourself also in the Lord,
And He shall give you the
desires of your heart.
Commit your way to the Lord,
Trust also in Him,
And He shall bring it to pass.
…Rest in the Lord,
And wait patiently for Him…"

Epilogue

What if there was more to discover, a different way, a better way for the stallion and his mares? Since their birth, 'someone' had been watching and waiting for an opportunity to reveal himself to them, to show them the better way. He was known to be wiser and more powerful than the stallion and his mares since he could offer all the comfort, provision and leadership necessary and more for their survival and enjoyment! The time had come. The stranger quietly and slowly moved in close to the herd, letting them sniff his scent while he crouched low. The wait was long, but necessary, to let the herd study him.

*Strangely, the intruder's movements were not like other predators, they were gentle and friendly, as if he knew all about them. At first there was resistance to his presence, but they discovered that he **was** like them, not a predator. The stallion was singled out for an invitation. This new unknown brought a strong reaction of fear and flight, which eventually gave way to the stranger's persistent gentleness and patience— a technique of advance and retreat—until finally a strong tug found its way to the stallion's heart.*

Understanding broke through and a new relationship was formed as the stallion turned to face his leader and willingly walked up to him. The 'join-up' was complete when the stallion slightly lowered his head and followed the Alpha out of the herd towards the hill where a new life was to begin with a higher purpose, with greater rewards and destiny fulfilled! The stallion found one greater than himself, one who was called 'comfort' and 'good.' Even though the stallion was free to come and go with his new partner in life, he chose to stay. His love was irresistible and compelling!

A Sweet Relationship

Freedom is an awesome thing! To some people, freedom means not being under authority or leadership. To others, freedom is not having to worry about life, and letting others do it for you. To many, freedom is making your own life choices.

Freedom can be defined differently by each person's situation. According to the Bible, the sovereign God gives each person complete freedom of heart to believe what he or she wants and to act on it, but there remain consequences for wrong actions. Some people can enter freedom more easily than others, but it is a free gift for all to discover God's goodness and love. We can use our gift of freedom to choose to 'join up' with Him, or to be independent and self-ruling. God never forces anyone to love Him, as true love is freely giving oneself to another without condition. He gives us freedom every moment to find our value and purpose in Him, or to find our value and purpose apart from Him. Freedom is a huge privilege with an awesome responsibility of how we use it. It is a test of the heart!

What does God want from us? He wants our heart and desire, so we can enter into a trust relationship with Him. The Creator knows what is best for us, and what His purpose is for our life. How can we know God's will for us? First, we need to recognize our need to 'join up' with Him as our Lord (Alpha) and Savior (Provider), and then we need to get to know Him by spending time with Him, called prayer. Intimacy with God is possible if we are willing to open up and work together in a partnership of trust and respect.

If you do freely choose to 'join up' with God, then when you give up your old nature of unbelief and independence from God for the new nature that is "in Christ," you will begin to experience a new and true freedom. You will be free from the power of evil, free from guilt, shame and eternal punishment. You will receive eternal life, God's forgiveness, His unconditional love, His power and provision and all spiritual blessings. Life with God does not mean all the bad things will go away, it means that we are truly set free to worship and know the One who created us for His good pleasure and purposes.

What will you do with your freedom? Who will you give your heart and desire to? It is only when you are in the Creator's will that you are truly free!

A Special Note to My Readers

Writing this book and having it published was just one of my childhood desires come true. I give God all the praise and thanks for its completion—after all, it was His idea! Writing this book has been a work of the heart, something I immensely enjoyed for the inspiration and motivation of causing others to know the one true God and to grow in the grace and knowledge of Him. I invite you, my readers, to let God capture your 'heart and desire,' because when you do, you will discover true freedom!

I would love to hear from my readers and would appreciate you sending me a personal response to my book by email. If you have any questions about the Christian faith, or my present situation with Rocky please forward these by email also.

tchoward@mars.ark.com

or

choward@gleemcanada.com

GLEEM Canada website:

www.gleemcanada.com

Printed in the United States
80758LV00003B/280-378